# AGORAPHOBIA

Robyn Vines was born in Melbourne in 1952, and grew up in
Australia. Her undergraduate training was at the University of
Melbourne and Carleton University in Ottawa; and she completed a
post-graduate degree at King's College, Aberdeen, in 1978. She then
worked as a Basic Grade and Senior Grade psychologist at University
College Hospital, London, for more than five years, before returning
to Australia in 1984. She is currently Assistant Director and Head of
Clinical Services at the Cairnmillar Institute, and lives with her
husband and stepson in Melbourne.

Robyn Vines

# AGORAPHOBIA

*The Fear of Panic*

Fontana/Collins

First published in 1987 by Fontana Paperbacks
8 Grafton Street, London W1X 3LA

Set in Linotron Ehrhardt

Made and printed in Great Britain
by William Collins Sons and Co. Ltd, Glasgow

To my parents,
and to John

# Contents

# Acknowledgements

For over nine years I have been talking to and treating many women and men with a fear of panic which has constrained their experiences in destructive and painful ways. They have talked to me openly about their difficulties in coping, and the effects of the problem on their lives. My first and greatest thanks are to them, for sharing their thoughts and feelings so freely.

I would also like to thank the team in the Department of Psychological Medicine at University College Hospital, London, for their help and encouragement in developing an interest in the area. I would particularly like to thank Judy Osborne for her support and supervision during the first years of my practising as a psychologist.

My warm thanks also go to the staff at the Cairnmillar Institute in Melbourne, and especially to Dr Francis Macnab, for enabling me to continue focusing on this particular area and to develop a Phobia Clinic specializing in the treatment of agoraphobia.

I am also profoundly grateful to friends and colleagues who have helped me during the course of working on the book, especially Felicity Bryan who encouraged me from the beginning, Bryan Magee who contributed ideas and suggested the title, Helen Fraser, Michael Fishwick and Judith Hannam at Fontana who have been constructive editors, and particularly Pam Balcam whose patient typing and re-typing and unfailing support during the process of writing have been invaluable.

Above all, my special thanks to my family, especially to my parents and to John, for their continual support, reassurance, and caring during the course of the project.

The author and publishers are grateful for permission to quote the following copyright material: 'The Autogenic Method of Relaxation' in Neidhart, Conroy and Weinstein's 'Autogenic Methods', from the series *A Guided Self-Management Series for Stress-Related Disorders*, published by the Western Center Health Group, P.O. Box 91542, Vancouver, B.C. V7V3P2, Canada; 'The Ten Golden Rules' from *Programmed Practise for Agoraphobia* by Mathews, Gelder and Johnson, Tavistock Publications; 'The Life Line Concept' from *Social Skills and Personal Problem Solving: A Handbook of Methods* by Priestly, McGuire, Flegg, Hemsley, and Welham, Tavistock Publications; and the four concepts of 'Face', 'Accept', 'Float' and 'Let Time Pass' from *Agoraphobia: Simple Effective Treatment* by Claire Weekes, Angus & Robertson Publishers.

# List of Diagrams

# Preface

The purpose of this book is to help all those who suffer to any degree from a fear of panic and agoraphobia. I have written it for people who are affected or constrained by anxiety, which they themselves may not understand, when confronted with normal, everyday tasks, such as getting out of the house, travelling on buses, tubes or trains, shopping, going in a lift or flying – activities which other people take for granted. These people are seized by such panic that they feel unable to cope. They find their lives are disrupted by this fear of panic, frequently to such an extent that their activities become curtailed and every movement is accompanied by fearful calculations about whether they can survive the stress.

It is now more acceptable for people suffering from agoraphobia to talk about it openly, to share and discuss it with friends, neighbours and fellow sufferers. Despite greater openness about the problem, however, it is surprising how many people, particularly professionals, remain ignorant of its causes and of the ways in which it may be treated. GPs are often the first people to whom agoraphobics turn for help, yet many do not know how to treat the complaint, how the problem develops, nor where to refer the patient for appropriate help. It is for this reason that, following more than nine years of working with people who suffer from agoraphobia, I have felt it important to present the means by which many people have been helped to overcome the problem. The aim of the book is to increase understanding on the part of sufferers and those who help them, be they doctors, psychologists, social workers, nurses, priests, volunteers, neighbours, friends or family, and to provide a self-help guide for learning to cope with and overcome panic, and replace anxiety and avoidance with confidence and courage.

The book is divided into three main sections: *Part I: An Overview* (Chapters 1–3), *Part II: Causes and Background Factors* (Chapters 4–7) and *Part III: Treatment* (Chapters 8–13). Parts I and III may be read separately, without close reference to Part II which is more detailed and technical. I suggest that those wishing to use the book as a straightforward self-help guide should read the first and last sections first.

For anyone suffering from agoraphobia, the techniques outlined will be of help in tackling the problem. However, more than technique is required. What is needed most of all is the genuine desire to get well, and the motivation and determination to succeed. If these are present, then you have a definite chance of overcoming your fear.

Robyn F. Vines
1987

*Part I*

# An Overview

*Chapter 1*

# The Fear of Panic and Agoraphobia

I had my first panic attack eighteen months ago when I was thirty-nine years old. It was like a giddy turn, but much worse. My heart was pounding, I couldn't get my breath and my legs were shaking so much that I felt I was going to fall down. I was working at the time and the only thing I could do was to go and lie on the floor in the ladies' toilet until it had passed. I went to the doctor and he put me on drugs: melleril, diazepam and iron tablets. They didn't help and the situation got worse. I had to stop work and found that I was beginning to avoid things and staying home more than I should. Then, six months ago, I awoke in the middle of the night and found that I couldn't breathe. My husband called an ambulance and they took me to hospital where I stayed a week. There was no need for it. They said it was anxiety and I now know that it was. After that, I found I couldn't go to church any more, or to the supermarket, shops, pictures, or really out anywhere. It was terrible and I felt really awful all the time . . .

Jane was forty-one when she referred herself for help. She had been under continual treatment with her GP since the onset of her condition, but the tablets he had prescribed had dosed her up and she had felt even less able to cope. A mother of four children (nineteen, seventeen, twelve and eight years old) and happily married, she had been a lively and involved member of her small town community prior to the onset of her symptoms.

## What is Agoraphobia? A Definition

Unknown to her, Jane had agoraphobia. The term refers to the experience of extreme anxiety or panic when walking out of doors, in large open spaces, on streets, in shops, strange buildings or when using public transport. It is the most prevalent clinical phobic disorder. The Diagnostic and Statistical Manual of Mental Disorders (D S M III) states that 'the essential feature of agoraphobia is a marked fear of being alone, or being in public places from which escape might be difficult or help not available in case of sudden incapacitation. Normal activities are increasingly constricted as the fears and avoidance behaviour dominate the individual's life.'

The term agoraphobia was initially used by a German named Westphal over one hundred years ago, although the condition itself had been observed for some time prior to this. He coined the label to describe the '. . . impossibility of walking through certain streets or squares, or the possibility of so doing only with resultant dread of anxiety'. The word used by Westphal to label this condition originated from two Greek words: *agora* meaning market place or place of assembly, and *phobia* meaning flight or panic. Westphal clearly intended the label to indicate a fear of public places or crowds, which is a central feature of agoraphobia as it is known today. Since its original use, however, the term has come to have a broader meaning. Agoraphobia now refers not only to a fear of open and public spaces, but to a condition in which a person suffers incapacitating fear away from the safety of home, particularly when in crowded or isolated places where escape and/or help is not possible. The fears may also extend to being on one's own at home.

Dr Isaac Marks in his book *Fears and Phobias* (Heinemann, 1969) states that a phobia may be defined as a special form of fear which:

1. is out of proportion to the demands of the situation;
2. cannot be explained or reasoned away;
3. is beyond voluntary control; and
4. leads to avoidance of the feared situation.

Agoraphobia, however, differs from other phobias in which the external stimulus is feared directly, for example phobias about dogs, snakes, spiders and moths. By contrast, the agoraphobic avoids certain external situations through fear, not of the situations themselves, but of feelings that rise within him or her when in these situations. It is the fear of being overwhelmed by feelings of anxiety and panic which people think they cannot control, and the avoidance of situations through fear of these feelings, that characterizes agoraphobia. The internal stimulus is all important, as most people who experience these feelings are terrified that if they are engulfed by them again something disastrous will happen (for example, many fear that panic will result in a heart attack, a fainting episode, or loss of control in a socially embarrassing or mad fashion). They therefore avoid situations where help is unavailable.

Agoraphobia has a good deal in common, however, with phobias such as claustrophobia (the fear of confined spaces), vertigo (the fear of heights), and the fear of flying. There is considerable overlap between these conditions and many agoraphobics give support to the catch phrase 'If you've got one, you've got them all', so it remains puzzling why these phobias are referred to as diagnostically discrete entities. In all of them, there is an avoidance of specific situations through fear of being over-whelmed by panic and people frequently cope with their fear by avoiding such situations (for example, lifts, high buildings, aeroplanes), little realizing that, by avoiding them, they perpetuate the fear that their feelings will become overwhelming. People vary according to the situations which they avoid and this has probably given rise to the emphasis on separate labels. This differentiation is misleading, however, as it ignores the common fear of loss of control underlying all these phobias, and it is certainly inadequate for the numerous individuals who manifest fear in all such phobic situations. For example, many agoraphobics are claustrophobic (fearing lifts, etc), and they also fear both heights and flying. In addition, those who wear the label 'claustrophobic' frequently manifest mild to severe agoraphobic symptoms. The differentiation therefore remains somewhat arbitrary and it would perhaps be logical to find a new umbrella term for all these conditions in order to emphasize the similarities they manifest in the common fear of panic. A new diagnostic label has not, however, been formulated, so continued use will be made in this book of the term agoraphobia in its broader meaning, i.e. with relevance to those other manifestations of fear of panic. What is said about agoraphobia is thus also generally applicable to the conditions labelled as claustrophobia, fear of flying and vertigo.


FOUR INSIDERS' VIEWPOINTS

Keith is thirty-nine, a lecturer and head of department in a tertiary institution. He has been married to Sally for fourteen years and they have three children, two boys and a girl (eleven, eight and two). His symptoms had been bothering him for five years when he came for help:

> The problem is related to stress. I get panicky in situations such as lifts or crowds or in trains. Over the past four to five years there has been a lot of tension at work as a result of reorganization. I'm a very competitive person and I think the conflict has got to me. I've felt tense for a long time but it's become more extreme over the last few years. I now fear panic attacks, especially in places where there are others who know me and where I will not be able to escape easily to a secure base. I avoid any situations where I feel trapped, such as public transport, flying, sailing, a central seat in a theatre, going to a football match, and I get very anxious in the staff room and whilst lecturing or doing any public speaking . . . I also fear being alone a long distance from home where I may embarrass myself with colleagues. I'm frightened of losing control and of being admitted to hospital.

Katherine is fifty-two, married and mother of a son of twenty-seven and two daughters aged twenty-five and twenty-two. On referral she had been agoraphobic for twenty-seven years, since the birth of her first child when she was twenty-five:

> I remember feeling very depressed and isolated at that time, and twelve months later it snow-balled and I had to have live-in help . . . But when I think of it, I remember having my first panic attack when I was eighteen, and another one when I was twenty. It only caught up with me after the baby . . . Pretty much since that time, I haven't been able to do things on my own or go anywhere alone. I can't drive my own car, go shopping alone, travel long distances, go on holidays or be in strange surroundings. Things like going to the hairdresser's I can't do, because I can't stay put. I fear I'm going to have a panic attack . . . I would really like to be able to drive my own car, do my shopping, go away on holidays, and do anything I want to on my own.

Mike is twenty-five, single, works as a carpenter and lives at home with his parents. He has an older brother and sister, both of whom

18

have married and left home. When he came to see me he had been having panics for a year:

> I think my lack of confidence started when I was sixteen and began work. I felt pretty shy, and they were all married men who I didn't know how to talk to or take. I tried to be a part of them, but felt left out. I think I was too anxious for them to like me. I went away for a holiday when I was eighteen and came back to work feeling more confident. But one day everything kind of fell in a heap and my past confidence was gone. The only time I felt glimpses of that feeling was when we went and drank at lunch times. Friends I had were starting to get married and I felt a bit left out. I wasn't sure whether I was ready to have a girlfriend. Things got worse after that. Work was tiring and making me terribly nervous especially when I was sent a new fellow to work with . . . I had my first panic attack whilst I was smoking marijuana eighteen months ago. I thought it would only happen while I smoked, but it happened again while I had a hangover. Then it spread and now I can't catch the train to work or travel in the car outside city limits in case I have a panic. I avoid going to dark picture theatres anywhere, and I get anxious going to weddings where there are a lot of people I know and a lot I don't know.

Anne is thirty-one and mother of two little girls aged six and two-and-a-half. She has been married to Bob for eight years. She referred herself for help approximately one year after her symptoms began:

> I feel I'm agoraphobic. Whenever I go out I feel anxious and go 'funny' in the head. It started about a year ago when Jenny started school. We were having extensions done to the house at the time. I remember going to the supermarket and I got the feeling I was going to faint or collapse. It was horrible. It gradually grew to the point where going shopping became difficult, going out anywhere alone or where I don't know anyone, going to the doctor, and other things. I also fear heights. At present I can't get going or get interested in keeping the house tidy, or doing anything much. I just seem to start and then give way. I feel it is all beyond me. The main problem is panic and my fear of fainting. I feel trapped in a vicious circle. I need to get out but I feel I can't.

All of these people are agoraphobic. They differ, however, in the severity and duration of their symptoms. Their backgrounds also vary. All of them had sought help of some sort previously: Keith had seen a doctor for stress nine years previously, prior to the onset of his symptoms; Mike had seen a psychiatrist for two sessions, and had taken up yoga which he then dropped; Anne went to her GP soon after the symptoms developed and was given tranquillizers. Katherine, too, went to her local GP and was treated with drugs. Following this, and over the next twenty-five years, she also went to a psychiatrist (six years after the onset of the condition), two psychologists (one of whom saw both her and her husband for marital therapy, and the other for analytic therapy for five years), a hypnotherapist, an acupuncturist and, finally, a yoga teacher. She still had the full-blown agoraphobic syndrome on referral.

Most of those referring themselves reflect this pattern. The first port of call for help is usually the local GP, many of whom, either through lack of time or ignorance about the condition, prescribe drugs – usually tranquillizers. For many clients these serve as a crutch, but only in the short term and they do not tackle the habit of avoidance which develops in agoraphobics as a means of coping. Tranquillizers rarely help patients build a sense of confidence and control over their own feelings and lives.

## Frequency of the Condition

It is difficult to assess the exact incidence, though it is the commonest and most distressing phobic disorder met with in adult patients. It knows no barriers, and several studies have shown that there are no differences in intelligence and occupational or educational history between agoraphobics and people without the condition. In a study by Buglass *et al* in 1977[1], no differences were found in employment history, most social activities or family of origin in agoraphobics, when compared to normal, age-matched controls.

Estimates as to its frequency vary tremendously. Until recently, the most informative survey was carried out by Agras and his colleagues in 1969. They surveyed a small North American town and found that 77 people out of every 1,000 had phobias, and 8 per cent of these (i.e. 6.3 per 1,000 people) were agoraphobic. Of the 77 per 1,000, 2.2 were found to have disabling conditions requiring treatment, and 50 per cent of these were agoraphobic.[2] In his 1969 book on phobias, Marks reported that in London agoraphobia was the most common phobia presenting in a psychiatric setting, representing 60 per cent of all phobic patients. Phobic conditions were approximately 2–3 per cent of all psychiatric patients. Other estimates of the incidence of phobias differ widely in different studies from 60 per 1,000 (i.e. 1 in every 17 people) to 0.5 per 1,000 (i.e. 1 in every 2,000 people). Clarke and Wardman in their 1985 book *Agoraphobia: A Clinical and Personal Account*, estimate that there are between 20,000 and 40,000 agoraphobics in Sydney, Australia, and more than 100,000 in New York. Other experts maintain that more than 25 million Americans suffer from some kind of phobia (i.e. 10 per cent of the population), and of these, 15 million are agoraphobic (i.e. 6 per cent of the population). The most recent comprehensive survey done by the N I M H (National Institute of Mental Health) in the USA forms the basis of these claims.[3] Some other reports quoted in the press suggest a similarly high incidence of the problem. For example, Professor Grahame Burrows, Chairman of the Mental Health Foundation in Australia was reported in an article in the *Sunday Press* in Melbourne (19.8.84) as saying: 'four out of a hundred Australians are known to suffer from agoraphobia: 2 out of 1,000 people are so severely affected that they never leave their homes.'

With all these disparate claims, the incidence therefore remains unclear. Estimates range from 1 in 17, to 1 in 25, to 1 in approximately 170, and finally on to 1 in 2,000. (The latter two findings are likely to be an underestimate as the samples on which they were based were small: for agoraphobics are inclined to be secretive about their disorder and so may be under-reported in door-to-door surveys. Estimates based on out-patient statistics are also likely to be underestimates, as many do not seek help for the problem.) Marks and Herst[4] in a 1969 survey of 1,200 agoraphobics in Britain found it likely that at least one-third of agoraphobics never enter psychiatric or psychological treatment.

The true incidence of the condition probably lies somewhere within the range of the following estimates: the 1 in 17 found in the N I M H survey, the 1 in 25 claimed by Professor Grahame Burrows, and the 1 in 170 suggested by Mathews, Gelder and Johnston in their 1981 booklet *Programmed Practice for Agoraphobia\**. Whatever the frequency, it is a common problem. When I have talked to people about my work with agoraphobics, they have often responded by saying that they are related to, or know, someone who has the condition. There is a huge hidden incidence of the problem and it is important to realize that if you suffer from it you are not alone. Indeed, it is fairly likely that someone else in the shop or supermarket, or in your street, experiences the same thing to some degree.

Amongst the varying findings as to frequency outlined above, one statistic remains fairly consistent across studies, and that is the incidence amongst women. The bulk of the literature suggests that more than 70 per cent of agoraphobics are women. Possible explanations for this are discussed in Chapter 2.

## When Does It Start?

Whilst the disorder is rare in childhood, some researchers have found that approximately 21 per cent of their sample have experienced phobic symptoms as children. Panic attacks are commonly first experienced, however, when the sufferer is in his or her early to middle twenties, sometimes as early as late adolescence, but rarely as late as after the age of thirty-five. Marks and Herst in their 1969 survey similarly found that the majority of sufferers developed symptoms after puberty, with onset generally occurring between the ages of fifteen and thirty-five. Claire Weekes in her book *Agoraphobia: Simple Effective Treatment\**, also suggests that the majority of agoraphobics become ill in their twenties and thirties, manifesting the same range of onset as patients with diffuse anxiety states. Both conditions are seen by her to be a possible feature of young adult life.

On the other hand, some authors maintain that there are two peak ages of onset: at ages 15–20 and 30–40. However, these studies probably based their findings on too small sample sizes. Using pooled data, other researchers claim that there is a uniform distribution of onset age, this again occurring most frequently in the mid-twenties.

From this plethora of research, one thing is clear. The majority of sufferers seem to develop the complaint before the age of thirty-five,

Refer to Self-Help References (Appendix A).

and the condition seldom starts 'out of the blue' after forty. There can be exceptions, however. Jocelyn developed agoraphobic symptoms at sixty-one, soon after her 62-year-old husband had died suddenly and her 93-year-old mother had had a stroke leaving her bedridden. Jocelyn was grief stricken and it took eight months before she ventured out to the theatre again.

> A friend of mine had two tickets to *Hamlet* and asked me if I would like to go. I said yes, but when we arrived at the theatre and caught the escalator down to the level of the stalls, I was suddenly overwhelmed by panic and had to rush out and catch a taxi home again. I felt very insecure.

Jean, also in her sixties, claimed that she had become agoraphobic following retirement from her job.

> I had been looking forward to retirement, but when it actually happened I became more and more reluctant to go into town, and even to do local shopping. Finally, I found it very hard even to leave home. I guess I had been stressed in my job, and when I retired, it all caught up with me.

She had experienced surges of panic after the removal of the stress which she had coped with for many years, and eventually developed a pattern of avoidance to cope with her fear of these feelings.

Despite such exceptions, it often seems that people who claim a later age of onset retrospectively realize that they have been anxious or tense for some time, often for years.

## Duration of the Symptoms

In her survey of 528 agoraphobic men and women, Claire Weekes found that 60 per cent had been agoraphobic for 10 years or more, 27 per cent had had the complaint for 20 years or more, and only 27 of the 528 (i.e. 5.1 per cent) had been ill for less than 3 years. Most of her clinical sample were therefore chronic agoraphobics, whose history suggested their chances of spontaneous recovery were negligible. Sixty-five per cent had received previous treatment from one or more psychiatrists, and 30 per cent from their GPs only. Fifty-five per cent had received no help from their previous treatment; 6 per cent had been helped temporarily; 24 per cent were helped a little, and only 15 per cent had been positively helped, though they still needed additional help. Dr Weekes concluded from this that agoraphobia does not seem to be a transient condition.

Marks and Herst (1970) claim that results from their Open Door sample of agoraphobics (derived from responses to a BBC talk about agoraphobia) suggested that the average time which elapses before a person becomes handicapped is 15 months. The time it took for sufferers to seek help from different agencies after the phobia began was:

17 months from general practitioners;
34 months from psychiatrists (as out-patients or in-patients); and
57 months from religious and spiritual healers.

They also found that respondents reported an average of 13 years duration of the symptoms. Other researchers have found that 31 per cent of agoraphobics experienced symptoms for less than 6 months, 12 per cent had symptoms for 6 months to 2 years, 27 per cent reported symptoms for 2 to 5 years, and 20 per cent had symptoms longer than 5 years. Further findings suggest that the average duration of symptoms from onset to the initiation of treatment is approximately 5 years, and that the average reported duration of symptoms for females is 18.9 years (with a range of from 1 to 64 years), while for men it is 20.6 years (with a range of from 4 to 50 years).[5] Still more findings indicate that patients have a mean total duration of symptoms of 6.5 years before they begin treatment.[6]

The research results are therefore varied and inconclusive. Over the last nine years, I myself have found that the duration of agoraphobic symptoms in people referring themselves for help appears to have decreased considerably. Since returning to work in Australia in 1984, in particular, I have found the average duration of symptoms in clients to be markedly shorter than the above research results suggest. A patient I saw prior to my return from Britain, however, illustrates the much longer duration of symptoms which earlier was more usual.

Agnes was seventy-four when I visited her in her first-floor council flat. She had suffered from agoraphobia for forty-six years and clearly remembered the onset of the symptoms:

I remember when I was twenty-eight, we were evacuated to the country during the war. I had three small children at the time, and I had to walk two or three miles to the nearest town to do the shopping. I came over giddy and shaky on my way back one day, and I couldn't go out after that.

She had had several periods of remission of the symptoms, but had spent most of the past forty-six years in a state of terror about going out, or resignation that she could not. She had been referred by her local GP when she applied for medical recommendation that she be transferred to a ground-floor flat. She was terrified of going into the lift, or using the concrete stairs and of walking the length of the balcony in front of her first-floor flat.

Agnes had had her problem considerably longer than, for example, Keith, Mike, Anne, or even Katherine, who where discussed earlier in this chapter (46 years versus 4–5 years, 1 year, 1 year and 27 years respectively). Whilst this is a somewhat arbitrary comparison, it does reflect the growing trend towards shorter duration which I have noticed in my own patients. This apparently shorter average duration of symptoms before help is sought could be for several reasons:

1. People may refer themselves more readily to a community-based psychotherapy and counselling facility where I work now, than to a Department of Psychological Medicine in a large central teaching hospital, where I worked previously in London. It may be that a fear of stigma, and a wish not to be associated with psychiatric facilities, still operates to keep clients from seeking help as early as possible from non-community-based facilities.

2. There is now much greater media publicity about agoraphobia, and the number of informative books on the subject has escalated in recent years. People seem to be more aware of the problem, are able to recognize that they have an identifiable complaint, and know better where to seek help for it.

Again, a recent research study suggests that 'differences in knowledge concerning agoraphobia, and the availability and accessibility of treatment may all contribute to the reported discrepancies in the length of time from onset to contact with a therapist. It is likely that the recent upsurge of interest in agoraphobia will result in clients seeking help earlier than they have in the past.[7]

25

Whatever the reason for the apparent decrease in duration of patients' symptoms, be it a reflection of the different work-setting or of greater public awareness of the problem, there is room for optimism. We may hope that people will continue to refer themselves earlier, for it is frequently easier to assist in the early stages, prior to the syndrome becoming an entrenched part of the patient's lifestyle. Nevertheless, people with an extended duration of symptoms are also amenable to treatment and they should not refrain from seeking help because they have had, and coped with, the problem for a long time.

## Consequences of the Condition

If at all severe, agoraphobia invariably affects the routines of daily life in some way and has definite social consequences. For example, inability to shop, travel to work, collect children from school, travel to see friends; refusal of invitations; leaving of social gatherings before the end; imposition on friends and relatives for accompaniment, are all consequences of the condition. The findings of one study suggest that, in one-fifth of agoraphobics studied, the condition had placed a strain on the patient's marriage. The curtailment of activities and the involvement of the family (for example with shopping, if the woman or man finds it hard to go out), and the restriction of family holidays are some of the factors affecting family life.

Symptoms frequently elicit a good deal of sympathy, social attention and help from others. In the 1977 Buglass study it was found that husbands of agoraphobic women did the shopping and other domestic chores significantly more often than husbands of non-agoraphobic women. The husbands also said that they were adversely affected by their wives' symptoms and reported spending less time working than the other group of husbands in order to spend more time with their partners. The condition can therefore result in secondary gain for some sufferers, whose avoidance behaviour is reinforced by the social attention and support given by family and friends.

For other agoraphobics, however, the condition seems to have unrelievedly negative effects, resulting in severe depression and bewilderment about the curtailment of activity, and pervasively high levels of anxiety. Agoraphobia can be exceedingly debilitating and people sometimes report having thought of suicide prior to seeking and finding appropriate treatment.

For many, the consequences of the condition manifest both the negative effects mentioned above and the positive effects (including conscious and unconscious secondary psychological gain) arising from their symptoms. Both elements need to be considered if the person is to be treated effectively.

Many agoraphobic women are concerned that the condition will affect the development of their children, providing an environment in which the children can learn the fears themselves. Buglass *et al* (1977) found no evidence of any greater disturbance in the children of agoraphobics than among normal controls.* Mathews *et al* (1981) also concluded that there is no good evidence for any substantial detrimental effect of agoraphobia on family life, if routines like shopping, which are directly affected by avoidance behaviour, are excluded.[8]

The consequences of agoraphobia are, therefore, varied. Most individuals with the symptoms to any severe degree, experience considerable inconvenience as a result of the condition. For many, the support and attention received from others may result in secondary gain and thereby help to maintain the problem. For others, support seems an essential part of surviving the condition which can be, at times, intolerably depressing.

---

* However, it may be that in these control group studies individual differences reflecting fear acquisition in children of agoraphobics are ironed out. A few of my patients have reported learning some of their fears from their own mothers.

## Chapter 2

# The Women:Men Ratio – Are Women and Men Equally Affected?

Nearly all reports indicate that about two-thirds or more of agoraphobics seen by psychiatrists and other health professionals are women. This is true both in America and Britain, and the pattern seems to be present elsewhere.* Whilst some studies undoubtedly overestimate the percentage of women, the bulk of literature does suggest that more than 70 per cent of agoraphobics are female. Iris G. Fodor, in her 1974 survey of studies on agoraphobia found that, on average, 84 per cent of agoraphobics seen by clinicians were women, with estimates ranging from 64–100 per cent.[1]

One possible explanation is that the large sex difference in incidence may be an 'artifact' produced by women's greater willingness to admit fears and report phobias than men. This does not, however, explain the varying sex ratios for different phobias, and the high incidence of females amongst agoraphobics is surprising in view of the absence of such clear sex differences in other neurotic disorders: for example, in anxiety neurosis and social anxieties, which are found to be equally present in both men and women.

An alternative, or additional, explanation may lie in 'physiological' factors. Some researchers maintain that mood changes associated with hormonal fluctuations during the menstrual cycle may account for some of the excess of female agoraphobics. The higher arousal level many women experience during their premenstrual phase may make them particularly vulnerable, at this time, to the acquisition of a conditioned fear response which usually occurs prior to the onset of symptoms in most agoraphobics.† In support of this, many women find

---

For example, in Australia I have found that more than 70 per cent of my agoraphobic patients are women.
† The exact nature of acquisition of agoraphobic avoidance behaviour is still the subject of much theoretical debate, but it is likely that the conditioning of fear plays a large part in most individuals.

that the severity of their symptoms fluctuates during the course of the menstrual cycle, worsening during the premenstrual week to coincide with, or reflect, premenstrual tension. A significant number of agoraphobic women also develop their symptoms after the birth of a baby – another period in which hormonal changes occur. Alternatively, some theorists suggest that this is a time when a woman might feel trapped in the marriage with young children to bring up – making a psychosocial explanation equally plausible. In relation to this point, an interesting feature of the study by Buglass *et al* mentioned in Chapter 1 may be noted: the thirty agoraphobic housewives studied, though they showed no differences from the normal control group with respect to other psychiatric symptoms or physical illness, had experienced more gynaecological illness. Indeed, 66 per cent of the agoraphobic women had required in-patient treatment for gynaecological problems versus 40 per cent in the control group. While these results are inconclusive, they do suggest that there may be some biological factor in the higher incidence of agoraphobia in women.

Of equal plausibility in accounting for the discrepancy between men and women is the 'Sex-Role Theory'. This is outlined in Iris G. Fodor's 1974 article 'The Phobic Syndrome in Women', where she argues that socialization, sex-role stereotyping, and sex-role conflict are responsible for the more frequent female development of agoraphobia. She states:

> For males, socialization tends to enhance experimental options . . .
> for women, the socialization process tends to reinforce the
> nurturant, docile, submissive and conservative aspects of the
> traditionally defined female role, and discourage personal qualities
> conventionally defined as masculine: self-assertiveness,
> achievement orientation, and independence.

Fodor goes on to suggest that adult women's alternatives to mature autonomy in relationships are obedience ('to lord and liege'), flight, and phobia; the latter reflecting an exaggeration of the stereotypic feminine role (avoiding autonomy, initiative and assertiveness). She points out that, under the realistic stresses of adult life, many women become anxious, wish to flee their relationships and be independent. In reality, however, they become phobic: a solution which reflects their own form of socialization and lack of preparedness for independent action.

There are now many books on the market which analyse and try to counteract the difficulties which women find in becoming independent. Collette Dowling's *The Cinderella Complex* and Penelope Russianoff's *Why Do I Think I Am Nothing Without A Man?* are two of the better known examples. Another book of this kind is Maggie Scarf's *Unfinished Business*, which was published in 1980. The author entitled one of her chapters 'Femininity as a Symptom', and in it she argues that the personality traits and characteristics associated with 'being feminine' are in themselves pathogenic.* She discusses a study by Broverman *et al* (1970) in which mental health professionals were asked to assess and list behavioural traits of a 'healthy male', a 'healthy female' and a 'healthy adult'. It was found that there was a discrepancy between the 'healthy adult' and 'healthy female'. For example, some traits which were rated as being appropriately 'feminine' – such as less aggression, less dominance, more freedom of emotional expression and more excitability – were not seen to be consonant with emotional well-being in the 'healthy adult' individual.† The 'feminine' role implied pathological tendencies, and the results suggested that being 'normal' and being 'normally feminine' were not quite the same thing. Scarf goes on to argue that the line between 'neurotic' dependency and the 'normally higher' needs characteristic of feminine dependency is a difficult one to draw. Passive dependent behaviour is encouraged in females but rarely tolerated in males; women are also generally perceived to be more dependent than men.

Thus, in the light of the marked predominance of female agoraphobics, it may be that these culturally determined and socialized dependent behaviours in women set the stage for the development of a sense of helplessness and fearfulness, from which agoraphobic avoidance symptoms develop. For there does seem to be a good deal in common between the symptoms and stereotypically feminine behaviour.

* i.e. causing pathological symptoms. Scarf, viewing the higher incidence of depression in women, wonders if feminine personality traits are in themselves 'depressogenic'. As we have seen, the sex-role theory of agoraphobia argues that they are certainly 'agoraphobia-genic'.

† Questions can obviously be raised about some of these findings (e.g. the notion that the 'feminine' trait of more freedom of emotional expression is not consonant with emotional well-being). However, the conclusions are nonetheless interesting.

Fodor (1974) invokes this 'dependent' feminine sex-role stereotype as the main factor explaining the higher frequency of agoraphobia in women and she claims that parental, school and media influences are all responsible for perpetuating this pathogenic female dependency. On the other hand, Emmelkamp (1979) argues that sex-role stereotyping is not such an important factor in the development of agoraphobia, but is much more so in maintaining it.[2] Nevertheless, most other researchers, like Fodor, see traditional roles as important in both the development and maintenance of the condition, as well as in explaining the discrepancy in frequency between the two sexes. Claire Weekes (1977), for example, claims that the difference in sex-incidence is understandable because agoraphobia develops naturally in women, whose work at home gives them an opportunity to shelter there if they so wish. Men working away from home must make the effort to leave the house daily and therefore do not develop the condition so easily. Although it is estimated that as many men as women suffer from anxiety, being obliged to travel to and from work each day means that relatively few men suffer full-blown agoraphobic symptoms. Instead, a man may express the agoraphobic phase of an anxiety state in a reluctance to travel from his home town or to sit through business meetings where he feels trapped. Weekes labels this condition as the 'city-bound executive syndrome', in which flying, or extensive travel to outer districts and other cities is avoided, and promotion is refused if it means more travel. This type of problem is quite frequent in men and freedom of movement is greatly curtailed by it. Indeed, I have seen many men who have turned down promotional opportunities because of their fear of flying and travel.

Returning now to the social roles of women, some theorists have used the label 'housebound housewives' to describe agoraphobics, because of the preponderance of married women at home amongst identified agoraphobic sufferers. Claire Weekes found in her sample of 528, that 486 (i.e. 92 per cent) were women, of whom 89.5 per cent were married. Seventy-eight per cent of the women were involved in 'home duties', 12 per cent in part-time work, and only 10 per cent in full-time work. In comparison, 52.4 per cent of the 42 men were married, and only 5 per cent of the men had retired.

Again, Marks and Herst found that 95 per cent of the 1,200 respondents to their survey were women; of these 80 per cent were married, and the proportion who worked was lower than in the general population. Sixty per cent indicated that they would prefer to work outside the home. This particular group, referred to as 'discontented housewives', reported more severe phobias and other psychiatric symptoms; their phobias affected them more and were worse when they were alone; they also had more fears of being alone than the other agoraphobic women who reported being content at home. They needed more help and were often unable to obtain it; they were more depressed, more exhausted and irritable, and had more neurotic symptoms. Surprisingly, this same group described themselves as more sociable, less anxious and more independent prior to the onset of their symptoms than did those women who were content with remaining at home.

Such data, however, do not establish a causal connection between not working and agoraphobia, because it remains unclear whether not working caused more pathology and discontent amongst this group, or whether their more severe symptoms prevented them from working and developing contacts outside the home. In fact, this type of chicken-and-egg circle is characteristic of most agoraphobics, and not only 'housebound housewives'. The symptoms may result in less activity, which then causes a worsening of the symptoms. Alternatively, less outside activity (for example, after the birth of a baby, or being made redundant) may result in the onset of the symptoms.

In conclusion, it appears that several factors might interact in determining phobic behaviour and in producing a statistically greater percentage of women sufferers in the various surveys. The figures may, in part, be an artifact, and may also reflect biological differences, and certainly social differences, between women and men. It is not, however, only housebound housewives who suffer from the complaint, as the next chapter makes clear. Agoraphobia seems to affect many people, both men and women, in all walks of life.

The previous discussion illustrates clearly that, in the area of agoraphobia, dogged adherence to any one theory does not fully explain all features of the complaint. This is particularly apparent when we try to analyse each individual's reasons for developing their symptoms and to describe the different ways in which people can be helped. If you wish to use this book to help you understand the development of your own agoraphobia and tackle the symptoms, then read the next chapter and move straight on to Part III, which outlines practical techniques. You can return to Part II if you wish to have a more theoretical understanding of the condition.

## Chapter 3

# Three Case Histories

## Jenny's Story

*The problem:* Jenny was forty-two when she came to see me. She had been agoraphobic for three-and-a-half years and was in danger of losing her job as secretary and personal assistant to the recently retired chairman of a large international company, for whom she had worked for the past twelve years. She had sought help from a clinical psychologist eight months after the onset of her symptoms and, whilst she received help in other areas of her life during the two years she had attended sessions, the symptoms had continued to get worse. She had also seen a psychiatrist for two months two years after the problem began, to no effect; and she had attended a one-week residential behavioural programme for agoraphobics one year prior to her being referred to me. None of these contacts had removed the symptoms and she was extremely depressed on referral, so much so that she had contemplated suicide on several occasions. In her first session she outlined the problem:

> I think I have agoraphobia. I have all the symptoms. I've read Claire Weekes' books and they've helped me to understand, but they haven't helped me over the problem . . . the symptoms struck about three-and-a-half years ago. I remember one lunch time I walked out for lunch in Oxford Street and I was standing at the corner of Baker Street when I suddenly felt faint. I headed on down the street – I can't remember the exact course of things – and found a café where I collapsed and had a cup of tea. I was shaking like a leaf. After that, whenever I went out from work the same thing happened. I had two months off because of the shaking which also started to occur in the office. I felt safe at home, but it seemed to come back at work. I can't remember in detail the rest of that year. I know that later I wasn't able to drive, but I have been able to get

back to that thank heavens. The next two years were pretty similar to the first. I've continued working but it's been very stressful . . . Now, because of the problem, I find that I can't play squash any more (which I used to do twice a week). I avoid going to the theatre, meeting other people, waiting in queues or in almost any situation. (I hate waiting at red traffic lights and try to avoid routes with traffic lights as much as possible.) I avoid visiting hospitals (which I fear) and I find I can't go into most shops because of it. I also miss contact with my workmates very much as I am unable to go out or join them in other activities without fear. I frequently fear having a panic attack and also fainting or falling over when I get very shaky legs. I am also frightened that if I do not conquer my present problems, change of life may be very difficult for me . . . I would dearly love to be able to go into shops again, even just stand, without shaking or trembling. I would also like to be able to go to theatres without the same thing happening, and I would like not to be afraid to talk to other people. Basically I would like to regain my self-confidence.

*Biography*: Jenny was an only child, born when her mother was thirty-two and her father thirty-three. When asked about her background, the first thing she recalled was when she was three:*

I remember playing with a black mammy doll. I was called inside and left the doll outside. It was stolen and I got into trouble. I was told I wouldn't get another one . . . In the early years, my father's mother lived with us. She loved me very much, as I did her. She looked after me and I felt a great sense of loss when she died . . . When I was ten my mother used to teach other girls to play tennis. I used to have to chase the balls and throw them back. She didn't teach me until later . . . When I was about twelve, I learnt about sex from my parents but after that it was never discussed . . . At thirteen, and all through my teenage years, girlfriends of mine had boyfriends and I was not allowed to. My parents did not welcome outsiders into the home and I was not allowed to go out to meet people socially (except at the church). My upbringing was always to do as I was told. Most times I used to do this, even though as I grew

* Refer to Chapter 11 for the approach to biographical material.

up it was sometimes against my wishes. My father was very strict, as was my mother, and I had to abide by his rules. If I didn't obey his instructions I was punished. (My parents get along well. My mother is the dominant partner, and Father usually gives in to her.)

. . . When my parents considered it was time for me to meet someone they asked friends if they knew anyone suitable. The person who was suggested suited my parents but did not suit me. Very difficult years followed, as I was virtually being forced to go out with someone I did not wish to. If I did meet anyone else, they were not made welcome at home and therefore they did not continue to see me . . . When I was twenty I met a man at work who taught me a lot about life I did not know about. He helped me in many ways to broaden my outlook and to take steps I would not otherwise have taken. He continued to support me until I was about twenty-eight when I changed jobs . . . I met Martin, my husband-to-be, when I was twenty-two, and he was twenty-eight. He was a food and drink waiter and was married at the time, and my parents disliked him and his parents. He didn't have any money and had to go through the divorce . . . The family friction was very upsetting to me and I tried very hard with both sides over many years to put relationships on a better footing. My efforts were in vain and it took a lot out of me emotionally. This went on for about ten years. I was also working very hard at my job. When I was twenty-eight a friend of mine (an old lady) was selling her flat. I bought it from her and moved out from home. This gave me more freedom to be 'myself'. I kept in touch with my parents and visited them once a week. I also changed jobs at about this time and started work with the company I am with now . . . When I was thirty, I was offered the position of Secretary to the Managing Director. I did not readily accept the position, but was persuaded to do so by my boss at the time. After a few years my new boss was appointed Chairman of the company. Working for him in these positions involved me in years of top-level, high pressure work, which I am sure contributed to my present state of health . . . (He is now retired but I continue to work for him five days a week. I would like to work for him, say, four days a week, but he will not agree to this.)

. . . When I was thirty-four my closest girlfriend from work and her husband moved to Canada. I felt a tremendous loss at this, as she was someone I could confide in . . . For many years while at work, my main interest was playing squash (pennant and social). I enjoyed this and miss it now that I am not well enough to play (I lack sufficient energy, and I fear the panics) . . . When I was thirty-six, Martin and I finally married, because it was what we both wanted. Our parents then had to accept the situation. We bought and moved into our own home the following year. (We're both very happy in it.) . . . A year later it was broken into and I came home to find what had happened, as my husband was at work that night . . . On two separate occasions my husband was out of work for short periods. His mother felt ashamed of him at these times and made things difficult for him. It was a difficult situation for both of us to cope with. It was at about this time that I had my first panic attack. Not long after, my father-in-law developed cancer. He suffered for ten months before his death and it was emotionally very difficult for me to cope with hospital visiting, etc. on top of my very busy job . . . Last year (the year following his death) my mother-in-law told my husband she wanted nothing more to do with us. I have not seen her since. Both of these events have upset both of us very much . . .

In view of her history, it is not surprising Jenny became agoraphobic. Her story is one of cumulative tension, which finally surfaced in panic and the consequent fear of panic in her thirty-eighth year. Whilst she was growing up, her parents were overprotective and at times unloving, leaving Jenny with ambivalent feelings about them which made her feel guilty. She grew to resent their intrusive strictness which left her little autonomy to make her own decisions. Not having been taught or encouraged to be assertive, she gave way to their wishes, bottling up her feelings of anger and resentment. She felt perpetually caught between the conflicting pulls of her own wishes and her duty to them. None of this contributed to a sense of confidence. The prolonged family friction over her relationship with Martin, pressure at work, the additional stresses of losing her best friend, the burglary and Martin being out of work, all contributed to her anxiety and the ultimate emergence of panic. The pressure did not abate and this, together with the spiralling fear of the panic itself, led to the frightened, shaky, depressed and unconfident state in which Jenny referred herself three- and-a-half years later.*

For a discussion of Jenny's treatment refer to Chapter 13.

# Liz's Story

*The problem:* Liz was forty-three when she came for help. She was a married housewife, mother of a boy and two girls (aged sixteen, fifteen and eleven). On referral, she had been agoraphobic for nine years. There had been some remission of symptoms during this time, but they never fully went away and reemerged in full force six months prior to my seeing her. After the initial onset, she went to her local GP and was treated with drugs. During the next eight years she went for help to a psychiatric clinic, a naturopath, a faith healer, another psychiatric clinic, a doctor who practised alternative medicine and to a person teaching meditation techniques. She still had the full-blown agoraphobic syndrome on referral. In her first session she described her symptoms as follows:

> I remember nine years ago returning from shopping in town and I suddenly felt terrible, as if I was going to die. My local GP put me on drugs and I gradually made myself go down the street again, until I got to the point where I was almost better – but not quite. We've flown overseas twice since that time and I've hated those trips. They were sheer hell, coping with my fear of panic all the way . . . The panic comes and goes. My heart bangs and misses beats and I fear that I am going to die. Six months ago I had a whopper and since then I've felt back to Base 1 again. I can't travel alone, I fear crowds, any social gatherings and entertaining, flying, and any trapped situation . . . I hate having this problem. It prevents me from doing lots of things. I feel angry and stupid because of it.

When asked generally about her life apart from the symptoms, she stated:

> I am far more withdrawn than I would like to be and feel that there is no real future. I am generally unhappy these days . . . I would like to be able to move freely in this world and go out to work so that I could feel financially independent and be extravagant without feeling guilty. I would also love to have a good marriage and to be able to stop worrying about my children . . .

*Biography*: Liz was the eldest of four, followed by a brother two years younger, to whom she is closest, a sister six years younger and a brother ten years younger. All are married and have three children, except the youngest who has two. She recalled her background:

I remember my father coming down the side of our house in his army uniform. I must have been only three. My mother rented out rooms to four elderly people and I spent a lot of time with an aunt who had a children's wear shop. She had no children of her own and loved to curl my hair and dress me up. I had a younger brother then, but spent most of my time with adults . . . I don't remember it being an unhappy time. Both of my parents were fairly strict, although when I think of it, not too much so. I always seemed to be a sickly child, with asthma, and I think I was overprotected and didn't do a lot of things because of my health . . . I started school when I was five and enjoyed that. I can recall it used to take me all my lunch time to eat my very small lunch. I ate very little . . . When I was six we moved into a house of our own. There were other children around and we just played and went to school. I feel that they were fairly normal years – and I liked school. I had another sister, then another brother. I don't remember anything startling over that period of time . . . I started high school when I was eleven. I did quite well until I switched to commercial studies in Form III. I didn't like it and left school after Form IV when I was fifteen. I went to work in a stockbroking firm in the city and for the next five years had a marvellously interesting time. I became secretary to the three partners, gained a lot of confidence and went to balls and parties, etc. . . . I changed jobs a few times before Tim, my husband, and I were married two days before my twenty-sixth birthday.

We immediately went abroad as Tim was doing further study. My son was born the following year, the same day that Tim started his first job . . . We moved a few days after the baby was born and that was fairly traumatic, as I didn't know anything about babies and I knew no one in the vicinity. We had rather a damp house with one open fire and I will always remember the cold. I was very depressed and it was a good four months before I think I spoke to anyone else there, apart from the doctor that I registered with. My husband played rugby and met a fellow who had a wife with two babies and he suggested we meet. All was well and we became firm friends. She was a bright cheerful girl and we had a lot of fun . . . I was twenty-nine when I had another baby. It was an easy birth and all was well, except that I was very homesick. I missed my family a lot. However, it was a time I wouldn't have missed. We were very short of money, but happy enough . . . We returned home in the same year. As luck would have it, Tim found a job in the same city as my parents, so back to the fold. We rented a house for a year and then bought one, and I made a lot of friends with play groups, kindergarten and a babysitting club . . . My youngest child was born when I was thirty-three and I wasn't too well with it. Nothing I could explain . . . At that time I had one child starting school and another starting kindergarten. I was busy, but had a few mod cons by then. My husband smashed his kneecap playing rugby and had to have it removed. He had to be driven around and taken here and there as it took many months before he could drive again. I also had a friend who went to university at that time and she landed her kindergarten-aged child with me. She thought I wouldn't mind as I already had one of my own there! She also had an older boy who was on drugs and in a lot of trouble and she would spend hours pouring out her problems to me. I also had another friend who started relief teaching and I seemed to have landed the job of minding her four-year-old, too. Her two older children would come to my place after school and then she would arrive and tell me all about the problems she had had at school all day. I didn't seem to have any time to breathe! It was during this time, when my youngest was less than a year old, that I had that first terrible panic on my way home from shopping. I was treated with drugs and they helped a bit, but not much. It gradually became a bit better, although it was there all the time from then on . . . They were difficult years.

Eighteen months later my husband was posted overseas again for three years. We didn't hesitate to go. It was a different lifestyle altogether. There were a lot of problems to start with as we couldn't find any housing and things were very expensive. Also, the children couldn't start school for four months as the school year was different. After that, I had a good rest really and enjoyed that part of it . . . My husband worked day and night and weekends for months.

40

He had a big job and we played second fiddle to that. (That was the norm over there.) I knew a lot of people and the children had excellent schooling and did every extra activity that we could think of. We took our home leave after eighteen months and how I got on the plane I will never know. But I had no choice. The trips were living hell, even though I enjoyed the holiday once I got there.

We moved back home after three years and moved house – only a few blocks away. I was thirty-nine then . . . Feeling OK but not 100 per cent by any means . . . We had a big party when my husband turned forty. 'Life begins at forty', he said. Two months later he had cancer, a large tumor which they opened up and closed up again. Radiotherapy and chemotherapy treatment lasted ten months. We all handled it well. I was good – quite strong really. He worked most of the time and we had great support from his company. We managed very well and went out and had visitors in and led a fairly normal life really. The kids were fine . . . He is well now and hopefully will continue to be so. I've tried to talk to him about it but he says it doesn't worry him a bit . . . That was three years ago now . . . About six months ago, I had a part-time job which was very busy. I had a few bad panic attacks but kept at it. Then I had the worst attack I'd had for ages. Too many things to do for Christmas and things became worse, so I started my search again for the cure. I went to a psychiatric clinic but got worse and was so bad at times I didn't want to go out at all. I was feeling very depressed about the whole thing. I quit my job . . . and miss the money, little as it was. I miss the commitment of having to go there too . . . I hope there are better things ahead. I count my blessings often, but it doesn't help.

Again, the picture is one of cumulative tension and stress. Overprotected as a child, and unconfident at school, Liz nevertheless coped well after starting work and enjoyed the period before she was married. After the birth of her first child, however, she was isolated and depressed for quite some time, having to deal with a new country and lack of friends. Again, she managed to cope well after a while, but bottled up feelings of resentment, particularly against her husband for not having supported her as she would have liked, which stayed with her during the following years. Overt tension emerged once more some years later after the birth of her third baby when her husband was dependent on her after an operation and several of her friends made heavy demands on her. She was unable to be assertive and consequently was left with responsibilities she found difficult to handle. At this time, the panic emerged and for the next nine years extra pressures (for example, her husband's cancer) took their toll. In addition, the fear of panic itself created a vicious circle of panic, avoidance, lower self-confidence and further panic under pressure, leading, with the other stresses, to a lower sense of self-esteem, all of which contributed to Liz's frightened and depressed state.*

## Peter's Story

*The problem*: Peter was forty when he referred himself for help. He was married with two daughters (twenty and thirteen) but had separated from his wife eighteen months previously. He worked as an accountant.† His first panic attack had occurred twelve months earlier. Since that time he had been to see three separate doctors and had attended stress management classes. Both he and his wife had received marriage counselling for approximately six months after their separation. In his first session he outlined his difficulties:

> I seem to be in a constant state of fear and anxiety in most things I do. I also get physical symptoms such as palpitations, tingling hands and feet, together with the panic attacks which I am unable to control. In a nutshell, I have a fear of fear. I also have a fear of being alone . . . I don't know what is causing these problems except, as they started last year, they would probably be related to the problems Susan, my wife, and I have been having for the past eighteen months . . . Of late, I seem always to be in a depressed state, so much so I think to myself if only I could feel happy and not have these constant physical symptoms. I frequently fear I'm going to have a panic attack and consequently I'm scared of being by myself. I have a fear both of ill health and of dying. Because of these feelings I'm anxious about, and trying to avoid, meetings at work, having people round for dinner, going out to functions by myself, meeting people full stop. I believe that although these

* A discussion of Liz's treatment appears in Chapter 13.
† Peter exemplifies the 'city-bound executive' syndrome outlined in Chapter 2.

problems came to a head only twelve months ago, I must have had them for some time. I used to unleash my temper (which is a problem) on the family, and this enabled me to vent my feelings. Since our separation I have been unable to do this . . . I would like to try and stop avoiding things and people which at the moment bring on anxiety. I also wish I could stop being afraid of the numerous things which bring on so many physical discomforts . . . My goal is to stop worrying about my health and to get rid of my anxiety and depressed state. I would like to gain some sort of confidence which I hope will lead me to a normal healthy life.

*Biography*: Peter was fourth in a family of six: two elder girls and four younger boys (the age ranges now being forty-five to thirty-six). The first four children (of whom Peter was the youngest) were from their mother's first marriage. After divorcing her first husband when Peter was two, she married his stepfather, and they had two more sons soon after. The first thing Peter remembered was:

. . . the family going out on a picnic. I must have been five. I do know that if we wanted to go out somewhere it was a big deal because there were so many of us . . . The car stopped in the middle of an intersection and we all had to push . . . I had asthma as a child and was spoilt compared to the others. They used to resent this. I suppose the illness was a way of getting attention and what I wanted. For example, I used to get an asthma attack before going to a birthday party and then I didn't have to go . . . I can remember the last attack I had when I was eleven. It was very frightening . . . and then it just went. It disappeared . . . nothing at all . . .

. . . I started primary school when I was five and enjoyed this. We moved when I was thirteen to a new area where my mother was not very happy and my parents argued a lot, so after a year we moved back to our original town. Then we moved again two years later. We moved a number of times during high school and I found there were different levels from school to school. I consequently found myself trying to catch up with the other children. I didn't enjoy high school because of this, but I got on reasonably well in most subjects. In maths I always did well . . .

When I was sixteen I started work as a purchasing clerk. I met

Susan (my wife) a year later and this was a good time in my life . . .
When I was eighteen, the family went overseas because my father
was transferred in his job. I only went because Susan said she would
come. When she arrived three months later, she lived with my
family and was good company for my mother who had left two
daughters behind . . .

In the same year I started working with my present company, and
the following year Susan and I got married. Six weeks later she got
pregnant and that upset the apple cart. All our plans for working
and saving were blown. I felt a bitter disappointment and I blamed
her. We argued and fought a lot during the pregnancy. I didn't want
Joanne (our eldest), but when she was born she was a lovely baby
and life went on. We bought a house when I was twenty and
although it was a struggle, we managed. I worked a lot of overtime
for the next three years which did not suit Susan. I also went to
night school, and so put a lot of responsibility on Susan to bring
Joanne up . . . When I was twenty-three I was transferred to another
city with my job and didn't like the new town much. Houses were
very expensive . . . My parents were transferred abroad the
following year for three years . . . One year later Susan told me she
was pregnant again. Actually, she didn't tell me. She was too scared
to, and sent me a letter at work! Again I was disappointed and gave
Susan a hard time about it. I just don't like having a lot of kids
around. I think my anger about this pregnancy left a deep mark on
Susan . . . When Laura was born she was good . . .

My parents came home from abroad the following year, and
Susan and I moved into our new house and became more settled.
For the next five years (until I was thirty-four) we were reasonably
happy, although we did argue a lot. I feel it wasn't a bad five years in
my life. Susan joined a women's 'Toastmistress' club and seemed to
enjoy this . . . We then went abroad for twelve weeks' holiday and
argued the whole way. On our return, life went on much as usual.
Three years later (when I was thirty-seven and she was thirty-six)
Susan applied to university. I was genuinely pleased for her. She
spent a lot of time at university during the next three years. At the
end of that time we agreed that we should split up. We found we
were no longer compatible. This was two years ago . . . At about the
same time my mother died. I haven't mentioned this before, but for

the past twenty years she had a whole series of sicknesses from TB to having a lung removed . . . This was an upsetting time and even to this day I do not like going to her house where my stepfather now lives alone. Too many memories . . . I was very close to her. I think we built up a closeness during the years I suffered from asthma, and it continued later on . . . In the same year, Susan and I sold our house and separated. This was another sad time, although we continued to see each other. This was eighteen months ago . . . Initially it was a novelty living only with Joanne (I bought a flat and Joanne came with me, Susan went to my stepfather's, and Laura went with her), but this quickly wore off. Approximately three months after we split up, I went out with a girl, and two months later Susan started going out with somebody. It was at about this time I had an attack of palpitations and this started a whole new era of physical symptoms and depression which I've told you about. The following six months was a miserable time for me. I also turned forty which added to my problems! . . . Susan finished her university course and went abroad at the end of last year for a good restful holiday. I also went away to the sun and this was a big step for me as I went alone . . . (The previous two years had been the worst years of my life) . . . When Susan returned (early this year) she found herself a job which we're all pleased about . . . We probably will get back together . . . but I must try to rid myself of this fear and anxiety which I have constantly . . .

There are numerous background factors which may have contributed to Peter's anxiety condition. An underlying insecurity about his identity seems to have stemmed from his real father's departure when he was two. As a young boy, he was overprotected and spoilt by his mother, and at times used his asthma as a way of avoiding things he found difficult. Avoidance emerged, at a very young age, as a way of coping. Perpetual moving during high school undermined his confidence and his ability to achieve, and the final move abroad when he was eighteen made him ever more reliant on his mother and Susan: the two individuals on whom he was most dependent. The early and heavy responsibilities in his marriage started when he was nineteen, and seemed to result in frustration which he expressed fairly regularly in temper outbursts. This pattern continued for many years until

Susan started to make a life of her own and eventually left him. His mother died at about the same time. When Susan started to date someone else, Peter panicked. Both Susan and his mother, who had been his real sources of security, had abandoned him. The symptoms themselves then created further problems on their own, as Peter feared the panic and didn't know what had hit him.

These are some of the factors that account for the emergence of Peter's condition, and the frightened and bewildered way in which he referred himself twelve months after the onset of his panic.*

The above three case studies, and indeed all of Part I, indicate how intricate the web of causes is that leads to the onset of agoraphobia. For a more detailed discussion of background factors, the reader should continue with Part II. However, for those of you more interested in finding out immediately how to deal with the condition, I recommend that you turn to Chapter 8 and continue with Part III which deals with treatment.

Peter's treatment will also be discussed in Chapter 13.

# Causes and Background Factors

*Some Theoretical Considerations*

## Chapter 4

# Causes and Onset

Agoraphobia has received considerable attention during the last decade and a growing body of evidence suggests that new treatments can effect lasting improvements. However, according to Tearnan *et al* (1984), research aimed at understanding the etiology (or causes) and onset of the condition has lagged far behind treatment advances.

The three case studies in the previous chapter illustrate how complex the issue of causes can be. For a start, there seem to be at least three main components of the complaint:

1. the presence and frequency of spontaneous panic attacks;
2. the presence and magnitude of anticipatory anxiety;* and
3. avoidance behaviour,

as well as a high level of depression resulting from these. All three components may have different predisposing and precipitating causes. It is unknown, for example, why some individuals equally plagued by panic attacks do not develop agoraphobia, while others do. It is also uncertain why some people become phobic after a single panic attack, whilst others develop avoidance only after repeated panic attacks. Mathews *et al*, in a book entitled *Agoraphobia: Nature and Treatment* (1981), suggest that previously learnt styles of thinking and coping may determine whether a person suffering from panics will develop agoraphobic avoidance. Those who have learned to cope previously with fearful situations by avoiding them and depending on others – rather than through active coping and self reliance – are more likely to become agoraphobic.

The levels and types of causes and influencing factors are many and varied. Experiences in the distant or recent past may 'predispose' a person to develop any one, or all, of the three main components

---

i.e. anxiety and apprehension about the possibility of future panic attacks.

*Fig. 1* **Possible Underlying Causes in the Onset of Agoraphobia**

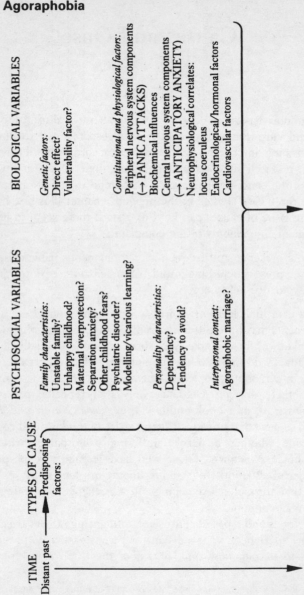

*BACKGROUND FACTORS*

**PSYCHOSOCIAL VARIABLES**

*Family characteristics:*
Unstable family?
Unhappy childhood?
Maternal overprotection?
Separation anxiety?
Other childhood fears?
Psychiatric disorder?
Modelling/vicarious learning?

*Personality characteristics:*
Dependency?
Tendency to avoid?

*Interpersonal context:*
Agoraphobic marriage?

**BIOLOGICAL VARIABLES**

*Genetic factors:*
Direct effect?
Vulnerability factor?

*Constitutional and physiological factors:*
Peripheral nervous system components
(→ PANIC ATTACKS)
Biochemical influences
Central nervous system components
(→ ANTICIPATORY ANXIETY)
Neurophysiological correlates:
locus coeruleus
Endocrinological/hormonal factors
Cardiovascular factors

TIME
Distant past

TYPES OF CAUSE
Predisposing
factors:

50

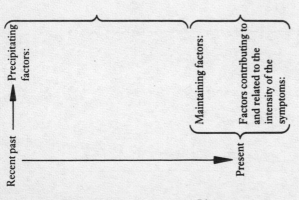

Recent past ⟶ Precipitating factors:

*Stressful events*
Relationship problems (Conflict at work and/or home)
Illness
Bereavement
Life changes (e.g. leaving home, engagement, marriage, pregnancy)
Birth of a child, etc.

PANIC ATTACK
(dyspnoea, palpitations, chest pain, choking feeling, dizziness, feelings of unreality, sweatiness, etc.)

Maintaining factors:

*Cognitive factors*
FEAR OF PANIC ('fear of fear' or anticipatory anxiety)
— Difficulty in attributing feelings to real causes

*Behavioural factors*
AVOIDANCE BEHAVIOUR: maintains fear
Lack of assertiveness
Secondary/Psychological gain

Present

Factors contributing to and related to the intensity of the symptoms:

*Variables causing arousal*
exercise
allergies
caffeine
sweating
hot weather
*Cognitions:* anticipatory anxiety
*Stress* (e.g. arguments, rushing, etc.)

51

mentioned above. Stressful events in the recent past may 'precipitate' the first panic attack, after which the way the person lives may 'maintain' the pattern of avoidance and fear which develops as a consequence. Additionally, biological factors may play a contributing role in determining which people are susceptible to panic attacks, given certain degrees of stress, and which are not.

In understanding agoraphobia, it is essential to avoid the assumption that there are simple unitary explanations. In each individual there is a myriad of intermeshing factors contributing to the emergence of symptoms. Some of the determining factors are present in all individuals, while some are not. In other words, a complex aggregate of causes is found in each individual. Fig. 1 summarizes some of the suggested variables which may operate to produce and maintain the agoraphobic condition.

As indicated in Fig. 1, there are two main groups of factors which may determine whether a person is vulnerable to agoraphobia or not: the psychosocial (psychological and social) background of the individual, and his or her biological contribution. The first group of factors will be discussed in the next chapter (Chapter 5), whilst the biological factors will be discussed in Chapter 6. Further, many different variables can precipitate the condition, and maintain it after its initial onset. These are also referred to in Fig. 1, and will be discussed in Chapter 7.

## Chapter 5

# Are There Psychological Predisposing Factors?

It is difficult to establish the specific life experience or personality variables that predispose individuals to panic anxiety and agoraphobia, although considerable research has been done in this area. Many of the studies are inadequate and there is no persuasive evidence to suggest any conclusive pattern of causes. Some factors seem to operate for some people, alternative ones for others.

## i. Family Characteristics

Different researchers have focused on varying features of agoraphobics' early family lives in an attempt to discover what factors may be relevant. One study found that there were more 'unstable family' backgrounds amongst agoraphobics than amongst other phobics (33 per cent versus 10 per cent)[1], whilst other research has reported that the fathers of agoraphobics were absent with unusual frequency.[2] On the other hand, further studies have come to the opposite conclusion – that agoraphobics generally come from stable families.[3]

Suzanne Shafar, in her 1976 study of agoraphobics, reported that for the sixty-eight cases investigated, just over one-third recorded a very unhappy childhood, with 12 per cent of them stating this to be the most significant underlying factor during the onset of the problem. But those suffering from social phobias recorded essentially the same proportion of unhappy childhoods as well.* Subsequently, Weekes (1977) found, in looking at conditions during childhood in her sample

There is frequently a considerable overlap between agoraphobia and social phobia (the fear of shaking, blushing, sweating, looking ridiculous or attracting attention by behaving awkwardly or fainting in front of other people). However, agoraphobia is focused more on the physical than the social consequences of panic (though the latter are seen to be important too). Consequently, different situations are avoided by sufferers of agoraphobia.

of 528 agoraphobics, that 75 per cent said their childhood was very happy, happy or passably happy – the remaining 25 per cent maintaining that their childhood was unhappy. The latter study, however, reflects one of the main flaws in work looking at background causes: namely that the research findings have relied almost entirely on self-reporting by agoraphobic people as the mode of assessment. Although this method is convenient, and often the only way of collecting information, there are certain drawbacks to it – for example, the problems arising from loss of memory or partial distortion of recall, as well as the social demands of a situation in which the person is asked about him or herself.

In further research, Buglass *et al* (1977), found that a significantly greater number of agoraphobics than controls came from 'anomalous home situations' (i.e. those which involved step- or adopted-relatives), even though there seemed to be no excessive conflict with parents. Conversely, some other studies indicate that agoraphobics may have a history of 'poor relationships with their parents', the deficiency of parental care being such that children are punished, criticized or denied the opportunity to be individually independent, so that they grow up viewing themselves as basically incompetent and unable to cope with many situations. Such studies suggest that these early experiences serve as significant predisposing factors in the development of agoraphobia and one investigation found that agoraphobics scored their parents low on maternal care. Nevertheless, the work of Buglass *et al* indicates no significant difference between agoraphobic and control groups in the frequency or 'type of contact' with parents.*
These authors did, however, find that twenty agoraphobics versus two controls experienced ambivalent feelings towards their mothers (a distressing mixture of positive and negative emotions), and had such feelings prior to the onset of their condition.

A much explored hypothesis is that parents, and particularly mothers of agoraphobics, are overprotective. Bowlby (1973), for example, argues that agoraphobic families frequently lack sufficient maternal affection and are dominated by an 'overprotective mother'.[4]

---

* One of the problems with control group studies, such as that of Buglass *et al*, is that they tend to iron out the importance of some of the factors, by reducing individual variations to group averages. It may be that the factor which involves the type of contact with parents is operative for some individuals but not for others.

Marks (1969) also described families of agoraphobics as 'stable, overprotective and close'. Further studies also indicate that mothers of agoraphobics, besides being overprotective, are more anxious than those of controls.[5] But it is not clear whether maternal over-protection produces fear in the child, or whether the phobic child produces overprotective behaviour in the mother. Only prospective longitudinal studies can answer this question.

Issues of family, and particularly maternal, overprotection there-fore remain unresolved. Certainly, with all of the clients discussed in Chapter 3, and particularly in the cases of Jenny and Peter, overprotection did appear to be a relevant factor. However, with many other individuals it does not seem to be particularly important in instilling lack of confidence or self-reliance at an early age. Several investigations suggest that some agoraphobic patients tend to have a history of 'separation anxiety', this being associated with the early loss of a parent.[6] Such an explanation is popular amongst clinicians, who maintain that loss can promote over-anxious attachment and fear of abandonment in the child, so predisposing him or her to develop anxiety attacks with possible threat of future loss. But, again, there is controversy about this issue for, to date, there is little empirical support for the hypothesis: indeed there are no controlled studies which clearly demonstrate a greater incidence of childhood separation-fears in agoraphobics than in those who suffer other conditions. One study, for example, found that 20 per cent of out-patient and 50 per cent of in-patient adult agoraphobics had a history of separation-anxiety, usually manifest as difficulties in attending school; but, as Tearnan *et al* (1984) points out, problems of school-attendance hardly qualify as definitive confirmation of separation-anxiety!

Buglass *et al* (1977) failed to find differences between agoraphobics and controls in their histories of separation-anxiety, and even if such differences had been found there would appear to be no clear-cut relationship between these early experiences and adult anxiety-states. Childhood separations due to parental illness, childhood illness, parental marital-discord, or wartime evacuation have all been found to be more highly correlated with adult de-pression than with anxiety symptoms. Thus, the role of this variable, like those discussed previously, remains unclear and, again, one is tempted to draw the conclusion that it may operate in some individuals (for example in Peter, whose panics seem clearly related to separation-anxiety), but not in others.

Other 'childhood fears' have also been studied in relation to agoraphobia and some authors speculate that the condition may be a reactivation of these, resulting from some stressful experience. Several investigations have shown the incidence of childhood fears and night terrors to be more frequent in phobic subjects than normals, and one study found that 60 per cent of a sample of agoraphobics had phobias as children. Similar findings have been obtained by other researchers.[7]

Another variable which has been analysed is past family history and prevalence of 'psychiatric' and 'psychological disorder' among the relations of agoraphobics. One study indicated the incidence of neuroses in the families of phobics to be significantly higher than in a control group of temporal lobe epileptics, while two additional studies found that 21 per cent and 40 per cent (respectively) of the agoraphobics investigated had psychiatric disturbance in their family. Solyom *et al* (1974) also reported a greater incidence of neurosis, alcoholism, and depressive illness in the families of mixed phobics when compared with the families of matched controls. On the other hand, Buglass *et al* (1977), after investigating the psychological illnesses in their patients' parents, found no evidence of an excess of psychological disorders in the family, nor of excessive drinking by the fathers. However, in comparison with a control group, there was a slight excess of agoraphobic patients with at least one phobic sibling. Furthermore, the brothers of agoraphobics were more frequently scored as showing 'psychological illness' (though chiefly of the non-phobic type) than were the brothers of controls. Tearnan *et al* (1984) states that it is difficult to evaluate the research in this area because of lack of consistency in the definition, assessment, and measurement of psychiatric and psychological disorders.

Some researchers have argued that 'learning' and 'modelling' patterns within the family are important causes in the development of agoraphobic behaviour. Bandura and Walters in a book entitled *Social Learning and Personality Development* (Holt, Rinehart and Winston, 1963), clearly describe the powerful effects of modelling, and some theorists and practitioners suggest that phobias can develop through social modelling.[8] The results of various early studies investigating whether children share their parents' fears are equivocal; however, one study found a higher incidence of dog phobia in parents of children who were afraid of dogs than in parents of children without dog phobia. A further study also showed correspondences between children's and mothers' fears. Mothers of phobic children had a significantly higher score on a Fear Survey Schedule* than mothers of non-phobic children, and both mothers and children were frequently fearful about the same situations.

Retrospective patient reports also provide indirect evidence in favour of the vicarious transmission of fear. For example, Solyom *et al* (1974) observed that mothers of 47 agoraphobic patients had a significantly higher incidence of phobic neurosis than mothers of control subjects (31 per cent versus 14 per cent); and Marks and Herst (1970) reported that 19 per cent of their group of 1,200 agoraphobics indicated they had a close relative with the same phobia. However, other researchers found that only 3 out of 45 phobic subjects studied reported vicarious learning experiences.[9]

Whilst several of these findings may suggest evidence for modelling (particularly by mothers) in the acquisition of phobias, a relationship between phobias of mother and child can also develop as a result of other processes – for example, genetic influences, as well as shared or similar traumatic experiences. In summary, therefore, whilst there is certainly suggestive evidence that vicarious learning can be held responsible for the development of some clinical phobias, definitive data are lacking; and, as with the other variables considered earlier in this chapter, it seems this factor may operate in some, but not all, agoraphobics.

## ii. Personality Characteristics

There is little or no agreement about early personality characteristics which might predispose people to develop agoraphobia. Studies of patients' personalities after the onset of the condition suggest a constant state of alertness, a tendency toward sexual inhibition† and an

---

\* An assessment instrument used to gauge peoples' level of anxiety in specific situations.
† This is by no means true of all, but of quite a number of agoraphobics. Buglass *et al* (1977) found a marked loss of libido in the agoraphobic group after the onset of the disorder.

attitude of passive dependency. Goldstein and Chambless in their 1978 paper 'A Reanalysis of Agoraphobia', claim that agoraphobics with panic symptoms present a remarkably consistent picture of non-assertive, pervasively fearful individuals, who perceive themselves as incapable of functioning independently. They also report sensitivity to rejection, disapproval and criticism, and a fear of decision-making and responsibility-taking.[10]

The work of Búglass *et al* (1977), on the other hand, suggests no difference between agoraphobic and control groups on objective measures of dependency; although self-reports and complaints of dependency were found to be higher for agoraphobics.\* The role of dependency as a cause is therefore unclear, particularly, as Stampler notes: 'it cannot be inferred (from subjects' self-evaluation of dependency once the disorder has already flourished) that these qualities are precursors to the panic attack and subsequent phobic avoidance. It is very plausible that the self-perception of dependence and low self-sufficiency develops secondarily to the debilitating panic symptoms.'[11] Nonetheless, by far the most popular hypothesis about the personality of agoraphobics is that they show two general behavioural dispositions:

1. Dependence on others, and greater dependency in general; and
2. A tendency to use avoidance as a means of coping.

## DEPENDENCY AND THE TENDENCY TO AVOID

In his thorough review of the phobia literature, 'Psychotherapy of Phobias' (1966), Andrews notes that phobic individuals are never described as self-assertive, independent or fearless, but are characterized by being dependent on others and fearful of specific stimuli; they also avoid most activities which involve self-assertion and independence in coping with stressful situations.[12] He speculates that, because of a degree of overprotection in childhood, the person learns a pattern of dependency on others which leaves him or her predisposed to the development of phobic avoidance later on. He further attributes

---

\* Amongst the findings on dependency in the Buglass study, no significant difference between the two groups in any of the areas of decision-making assessed was found. Criticism has been made of the analysis of data concerned with decision-making, in that the authors have tended to ignore discrepancies in the reports of the patients' husbands. The validity of their findings is therefore questionable.

the dependent style and subsequent phobic avoidance to maternal overprotection. Other researchers also hypothesize that agoraphobia is a reactivation of excessive early attachment behaviour caused by an overprotective mother.

Following a suggestion that dependent persons perceive reward and punishment as contingent upon some 'external locus of control' (i.e. upon people on whom they are dependent) rather than upon their own efforts, Emmelkemp and Cohen-Kettenis (1975) tested whether there was a relationship between fearfulness and 'locus of control'. They found a correlation between phobic anxiety and a measure of 'locus of control' as derived from a questionnaire, so providing some support for the dependency hypothesis.[13] It appears, therefore, that whilst agoraphobic individuals might prefer to experience internal control, they perceive themselves as more dependent on external or environmental control than upon their own efforts. Once again, however, the dilemma is to establish which characteristics emerge after the onset of agoraphobia and which are present beforehand.

Contrary to these findings, Shafar (1976) found an incidence of overt dependency in only 38 per cent of sixty-eight agoraphobics, thus indicating that dependent personality traits are not a necessary condition for phobia development. Claire Weekes (1977) also disputes whether there is a typical personality type peculiar to those who experience panic attacks and develop agoraphobia. Indeed, she argues that agoraphobics represent a cross section of the community and are not especially neurotic. Again, Isaac Marks (1969) states that some agoraphobics are active, sociable and outgoing people before the onset of the complaint. Only with the onset of panic attacks do they become increasingly anxious, afraid of venturing outside, dependent on others for support, withdrawn, retiring and so on, and it is false to infer or assume that they were like this beforehand. Marks also quotes Prince, who in 1912 noted that such phobias 'occur in people of all types and characteristics, amongst the normally self-reliant as well as amongst the most timid'. This attitude accords with my own experience of clients, who manifest a wide range of personality types and whose lifestyles and levels of coping beforehand can differ greatly.

### iii. Interpersonal Relationships

In examining the interpersonal context of agoraphobia, one is led to question whether there are one, two or several variants of the condition. Thus, in a 1973 paper, Goldstein listed four criteria which he believed characterized most agoraphobic clients:

1. female;
2. in a close relationship, usually marriage;
3. experiencing strong urges to escape this relationship; and
4. unable to initiate alternatives to staying in this unsatisfactory relationship.[14]

However, Goldstein later suggested in a 1978 paper 'A Reanalysis of Agoraphobia', with co-author Chambless, that agoraphobia is not a uniquely homogeneous entity. This paper maintained that a small minority of cases manifest 'simple agoraphobia' – in which symptoms of avoidance through 'fear of fear' are precipitated by panic attacks produced by drug experiences or physical disorders such as hypoglycemia* – while the remaining majority of cases reflect what the authors call 'complex agoraphobia'. The latter is composed of the following elements;

1. a central 'fear of fear',
2. low levels of self sufficiency,
3. a tendency to misconstrue the causal antecedents of unpleasant feelings†, with
4. the onset of symptoms occurring in a climate of notable and generally interpersonal conflict.[15]

Goldstein and Chambless suggest that the person's upbringing is responsible for this pattern, providing a climate in which it is difficult to

---

Many agoraphobics, for example, experience their first panic attack shortly after or during a debilitating episode of flu. Middle ear infection is also a frequent precursor of agoraphobia, since it induces unpleasant dizziness and lack of balance which causes anxiety. Even after the infection remits, dizziness can remain because of the patient's anxiety about his condition. So, if dizziness and lack of balance are amongst the first presenting major symptoms, a history of previous middle ear infection may well be suspected.

† For example, to attribute (incorrectly) the cause of a panic to external circumstances (e.g. a tram or train ride) rather than to the internal thoughts and feelings, or stress, which may be totally unrelated to the external circumstances.

acknowledge or express feelings. Such family backgrounds then give rise to later difficulty in recognizing and expressing feelings in a controlled or constructive manner, so leading to profound doubts in the individuals concerned about their ability to manage life and to cope with it. They therefore tend to seek partners who will take over the role of parents in looking after them. Partners who opt for this role are, in all probability, fulfilling dependency needs of their own. The relationship thus reflects a pattern in which neither partner experiences herself or himself as a whole, competent individual; and both are hoping to find attributes in the other which they lack themselves. Conflict soon develops (according to Goldstein and Chambless) between the agoraphobic-to-be's wish to become more self-determined and the simultaneous fear of having to cope alone. Peaks of anxiety (panics) occur when additional pressures are added to this basic inner conflict, and the fear of the panics themselves then leads to increased dependency. In addition, the partner frequently encourages this by protecting the sufferer from exposure to the external situations which have come to be associated with the panics – thereby reinforcing avoidance and again increasing the dependency which caused the conflict in the first place. This scenario represents what some clinicians refer to as the 'agoraphobic marriage': a pathological relationship between two disturbed individuals, which eventually results in the precipitation and maintenance of the agoraphobic symptoms. In order to test the validity of this concept, the pathology or otherwise of spouses must be assessed. Various studies have suggested that there is indeed a high incidence of psychiatric symptoms in the partners of diagnosed patients. This may, however, be a consequence of a selection process operating at the time of courtship (the 'assortive-mating hypothesis'), or a result of the experiences of living with a neurotic partner ('the interaction theory').

This 'interaction' versus 'assortive-mating' issue has important implications for treatment, for if the assortive-mating hypothesis applies, improvement in the patient may be resisted by the partner, since it inevitably disturbs the balance of such a relationship in which 'mutual overt psychopathology plays an important part'. Following these ideas, in 1977 Julian Hafner attempted to determine whether the marriages of thirty agoraphobic women and their husbands were best described from the assortive-mating perspective or from the pathogenic-interaction model. In fact, what he found were two distinct types of marital interaction among agoraphobic wives and their husbands, with the impact of treatment on these two groups being markedly different.[16]

Previous research had suggested that the way to determine whether or not the husbands of agoraphobic women are spuriously fortified by their wives' agoraphobia and dependence on them, was to examine the impact of effective treatment for the wives' agoraphobia on the husbands themselves. Some clinicians had already observed an exacerbation of marital problems after treatment of twenty-one married agoraphobics. They had concluded, however, that any causal connection between referral and deterioration in the marriage remained obscure.

In an attempt to clarify this issue, Hafner systematically studied a group of thirty married agoraphobic women and their husbands before, during and after a period of intensive treatment for the patients. Using mainly behavioural group and individual therapy, he was able to differentiate between two specific groups, categorizing these in terms of:

1. two main measures of symptoms (the Middlesex Hospital Questionnaire, and a Fear Survey Schedule);
2. a measure of personality (Hostility and Direction of Hostility Questionnaire); and
3. measures of self- and spouse-perception (yielding simple measures of self-dissatisfaction and spouse-dissatisfaction).

His findings were as follows:

*Group 1* were the most disabled. The agoraphobic symptoms were only one aspect of severe, general neurotic and phobic disability. The patients had high hostility scores and the results suggested that they tended to direct their hostility outwards to an abnormal degree (e.g. through acting out, projecting or criticizing others). However, husbands of these patients initially recorded almost normal hostility scores, and they also reported similar levels of neurotic symptoms to Group 2 husbands. (See below.) But three months after their wives' treatment, they showed more neurotic symptoms than before; and the primary impact of the patients' therapy on their husbands was mainly adverse. Two main factors emerged which seemed to affect post-treatment marital relationships:

1. The wife's determination and ability to overcome her fears during therapy; and
2. the husband's flexibility in his use of the psychological defence mechanism of denial (e.g. of hostility).

It became evident that the marriage was more likely to survive and accommodate continued symptomatic improvement, if the wife was determined to increase or maintain her independence and her husband was able to be flexible and relinquish aspects of defensive denial of his feelings. The marriage was unlikely to accommodate continued improvement if the wife lacked determination to improve and the husband was unable to relinquish his defensive posture. A third alternative was that the couple separated, or the husband became ill.* This seemed to occur when the woman was determined to continue improving and the husband remained inflexibly fixed in his attitudes.

*Group 2*, on the other hand, were less disabled, the agoraphobic symptoms existing in relative isolation. The individuals involved were less generally neurotic and had fewer overall phobic symptoms than those in Group 1. (Indeed, after treatment, the patients were less neurotic than the normal female population.) Both partners, however, showed abnormalities in their direction of hostility scores† – the husbands manifesting relatively high extra-punitiveness (directing hostility outwards), whilst the wives had abnormally high intra-punitiveness (i.e. self-criticism and self-blame for their symptoms and their failure to overcome their fears). The initial impact of the patients' therapy generally enhanced the well-being of the husbands.

Symptomatic improvement and its maintenance or increase after treatment, was found to be more common in Group 2; and the

---

* This 'yo-yoing' (i.e. when the agoraphobic partner improves, the other becomes depressed or ill in some other way) occurs quite frequently in the marriages of patients.
† See Hafner's paper for a clear outline of the direction of hostility indices.

results suggested that the pattern, or manner, of the husbands' use of psychological defence mechanisms had relatively little influence on the patients' overall response to treatment.

Hafner concludes that there appear to be two types of interaction between married women agoraphobics and their husbands, though he warns that the framework is crude and that there is considerable overlap between the two interactional types. His results suggest that married agoraphobic women should be considered as two relatively distinct but overlapping populations, with different patterns of symptoms and marital interactions; and he proposes that twelve months after intensive, graduated group treatment, women in Group 2 appear to be less neurotic than women from an age-matched normal female population. Such patients, therefore, 'do not conform to the clinical consensus about agoraphobic women. Far from being over-dependent, timid, emotionally labile and lacking in assertiveness, they appear, in fact, to be the opposite when they are free of the agoraphobic symptoms.'

To sum up, there appear to be several variants of agoraphobia, at least one of which seems to be maintained, if not determined, by the interpersonal context of the condition. The 'agoraphobic marriage', a pathological pattern of interrelationships between agoraphobic persons and their spouses, has been spoken about more frequently than it has been studied intensively. However, further work is now being carried out on this sub-group of sufferers, whose complaints seem to be inextricably connected with the interpersonal context.[17] Hafner's results suggest that, quite often, agoraphobics' spouses may initially resist a patient's symptomatic improvement, but that this is less likely to occur if the spouse is actively involved in the treatment. Hafner therefore believes that 'spouse-aided therapy' (i.e. treatment within a marital framework) is most appropriate for this type of patient. Nevertheless, Hafner gives several warnings:

1. He suggests that the two types of marital interaction observed in his study may not be specific to agoraphobics alone. If such interactions are found in other psychological disorders, this would highlight the fact that there are many aspects of the causes of agoraphobia, which so far remain unknown and which possibly lie outside the interpersonal realm.

2. Hafner also poses the question whether agoraphobia in men should be regarded as essentially similar to agoraphobia in women, or whether there are important differences to be taken into account. Despite the considerable work already done on male agoraphobics, this point still remains unresolved.

*Chapter 6*

# Are There Biological Predisposing Factors?

Several biological factors may predispose a person to the development of agoraphobia and these are discussed below under the two headings of: genetic factors and constitutional and physiological factors.

## i. Genetic Factors

In their book *Agoraphobia: Nature and Treatment*, Mathews *et al* (1981) review the evidence as to whether there is an underlying genetic influence in the development of agoraphobia. They conclude that the data lend no support to the 'direct-genetic-determination hypothesis'. Other research noting the incidence of similar problems amongst relatives reveals no evidence of increased prevalence of phobic illness amongst parents of agoraphobics, nor any significant differences between patient groups and controls.* Anxiety neurosis, on the other hand, has been estimated to have a family prevalence of 5 per cent in the general population; 48.6 per cent of children having one parent afflicted by the disorder were similarly affected, while, with two parents so afflicted, 61.9 per cent of children were found to suffer the condition.

Studies of twins, the most widely accepted method of evaluating the extent of genetic influences, again provide no evidence of agoraphobia being inherited directly. However, the evidence does suggest that traits of fearfulness and anxiety-proneness (which are elevated in agoraphobia) have some genetic basis; so it appears, therefore, that particular individuals may inherit personality traits (e.g. anxiety-proneness, or introversion) which can increase the development of agoraphobic tendencies. As Mathews *et al* maintain, these traits may reflect or create a 'general vulnerability factor', even though strong support for the idea of direct genetic transmission of agoraphobia is lacking.

* Also discussed previously in the section on family characteristics.

## ii. Constitutional and Physiological Factors

Liebowitz and Klein in a 1982 paper, maintain it is misleading to use the common term 'anxiety' to describe both panic attack and the agoraphobic's expectant/anticipatory fear of panics which results in avoidance behaviour. There is an underlying difference in these two processes and a proper distinction between 'panic attacks' and 'anticipatory anxiety' is necessary to any real understanding of the phobic process, for both are mediated by different parts of the nervous system.[1] This point is discussed in some detail below.

### PERIPHERAL NERVOUS SYSTEM COMPONENTS

'Panic attacks' are phenomena mediated by the peripheral or 'autonomic nervous system'.* Underlying the somatic (bodily) complaints of people who suffer from panics, lie a host of physiological changes.† Lader and Mathews (1970) noted profound and abrupt physiological activity accompanying the panic experiences of three subjects. Heart rate raced to tachycardic levels – at times too rapid to record; skin conductance was greatly increased; forearm blood flow increased ten fold; finger pulse rate increased and changes in blood volume occurred. All these changes reflected, in their simultaneous onset, marked autonomic nervous-system discharge, but once these physiological measures reached their peaks, they declined to initial pre-panic levels, so indicating that the attack was self-limiting.[2]

In formulating an account of panic attacks, Mathews *et al* (1981) state that: 'agoraphobics show an elevated level of autonomic arousal and an unusually slow rate of habituation. This physiological state enables an upward spiral of autonomic nervous system response, potentially resulting in a panic attack when a hypothetical threshold of arousal has been passed.' Further research has suggested that this abnormally high level of arousal in agoraphobics may result from a

---

* Autonomic nervous system: this consists of a chain of ganglia, running alongside the spinal column, with some ganglia in the skull connecting with the cerebro-spinal system. It controls the functions of smooth muscles and glands.

† I frequently see clients who say they have been told by others that their complaint is 'all in the mind': nevertheless, there are very real physiological changes underlying their experiences. What is made of the symptoms of panic, however, (ie. how they are interpreted) is, indeed, 'in the mind' and the patient's reactions have definite psychological consequences.

physiological malfunction in the arousal habituation mechanism (which normally controls excess arousal in most individuals), so leading to an overfiring of the nerve endings. On the other hand, Tearnan *et al* (1984) postulate that the base level of arousal of agoraphobics may be higher (than, for example, in simple phobics) because they have a greater variety of diffuse fear stimuli, which makes it difficult to avoid being affected.

Whatever the cause, a background of high generalized anxiety and autonomic nervous-system discharge seem to be critical underlying causes of panic attacks.

BIOCHEMICAL ASPECTS

Liebowitz and Klein provide details of research on substances which can artificially induce panics. It is commonly found that, while normal controls remain unaffected, intravenous lactate infusions will precipitate panics in patients who frequently suffer spontaneous attacks. This suggests that the patients may have a common physiological aberration, even though the mechanism of the action remains obscure. Further research is obviously needed to isolate those variables specifically required for the precipitation of panics.

It has been found that tricyclic antidepressant medications (specifically imipramine) can block spontaneous panic attacks in those who suffer from them, without affecting anticipatory anxiety. This is an interesting observation which supports Liebowitz and Klein's statement that the two forms of anxiety should be viewed as being mediated by different processes. Other findings from drug research:

1. the fact that antidepressant medications can block spontaneous panic attacks;
2. that panic attacks remain refractory to all classes of antipsychotic drugs which frequently are found to exacerbate the condition; and
3 that clonidine, an antihypertensive agent, can possibly reduce panic attacks by blocking sympathetic overactivity,

further suggest that biochemical factors do influence and/or cause panics. An additional observation that minor tranquillizers, such as Valium, though not blocking panic attacks, are quite helpful in treating the anticipatory anxiety of panic-disorder patients, again gives support for the idea of two separate, though interrelated, anxiety processes.

## CENTRAL NERVOUS SYSTEM COMPONENTS

### *Generalized Anticipatory or Cognitive Anxiety*

Panic attacks do seem to have a clear central nervous system component in that they are complicated by generalized anticipatory or cognitive* anxiety. As mentioned above, Liebowitz and Klein believe these anxiety symptoms to be qualitatively separate from the discrete panic episodes, although there appears to be some interaction between the peripheral-somatic anxiety of panics and central-psychic anxiety. Both may form a feedback loop; and once a history of panic attacks develops (or perhaps after only a single panic attack preceded by general chronic anxiety), the disorder can become self-perpetuating. The physical consequences of the attacks are then so pronounced, discomforting and alarming, that the patient develops an anxious preoccupation with them, dreading their next emergence and fearing insanity or death as a possible result. This anticipatory anxiety (centrally mediated) is reflected in cortical arousal which, in turn, affects the peripheral nervous system. The initial attack may therefore be triggered by centrally-mediated ruminative thoughts or images. Once this cycle is established, the heightened level of anxiety now contributes to a greater likelihood of sympathetic-nervous-system arousal and consequent panic attack.

### *Neurophysiological Correlates*

Electrical stimulation in the region of the locus coeruleus (a small centre of the lower brain which possesses the highest density of norepinephrine-containing neurones in the central nervous system) can produce a feeling of extreme fearfulness in humans. In contrast, damaging this small brain centre in monkeys has been shown to have the opposite effect: monkeys without a functioning locus coeruleus exhibit an absence of emotional response to threats and they display no apparent fear of approaching humans or dominant monkeys. Redmond in a 1979 paper has therefore proposed that the locus coeruleus may

i.e. arising from thought processes.

69

mediate physiological, behavioural and psychological aspects of fear and anxiety.[3]

## ENDOCRINOLOGICAL/HORMONAL FACTORS

Endocrinological changes are yet another class of physiological factors which seem to be interrelated with the development of agoraphobia.* Panic attacks have been found to occur within one year of oophorectomy,† within one year of hysterectomy, within one month post-partum, and within one week pre-partum in pregnant women. Some attacks, apparently precipitated by an event such as a pregnancy, are known to be mediated by simultaneous endocrinological changes; however, as one researcher states 'there is no evidence to discount the converse: that the psychological stresses induced by these situations alone may be sufficient elicitors of these attacks.'[4]

## CARDIOVASCULAR FACTORS

Recent reports have linked agoraphobia and panic to cardiovascular disorders and, in particular, to mitral valve prolapse (MVP). This is a generally benign cardiac abnormality occurring in 5–10 per cent of the general adult population and especially prevalent in young women. Research findings in this area remain equivocal, as only echocardiographic criteria (and not the clinical criterion for MVP, known as the midsystolic click) were used to differentiate between twenty-five agoraphobic women with prominent cardiovascular symptoms, and controls. Nonetheless, it does remain possible that benign cardiac arrhythmias, causing and perpetuated by anxiety, can lead to panic and agoraphobia in psychologically predisposed individuals. Palpitations may again be related to cardiac arrhythmias. All these findings are, however, by no means clear.††

* Some of the evidence regarding the influence of hormonal changes has been discussed in Chapter 2: see section on physiological factors as the basis for differences in incidence between men and women.
† The surgical removal of one or both ovaries.
†† It sometimes happens that individuals suffering from panic attacks with palpitations are incorrectly diagnosed as having MVP. This inappropriate diagnosis may then give rise to totally counterproductive anxiety, so exacerbating the symptoms the patient originally referred with.

# Summary

Research on biological predisposing factors suggests that there is no direct genetic determination of agoraphobia. However, indirect genetic effects on related personality traits may result in a 'general vulnerability factor'. Panic attacks do seem to be mediated by the peripheral autonomic nervous system which is often chronically over-aroused in agoraphobics. On the other hand, the central nervous system appears to mediate the general anticipatory and cognitive anxiety which plays a large part in causing and maintaining attacks. Both types of anxiety can perpetuate each other in a feedback loop: cognitive anxiety may precipitate the first panic which then leads to further anticipatory anxiety, which heightens the likelihood of further panics, etc.

Biochemical research suggests and reinforces the differentiation between the two types of anxiety, with some drugs (e.g. imipramine) being found to affect panic but not anticipatory anxiety. Conversely, minor tranquillizers are helpful in treating anticipatory anxiety, but do not block panic attacks. Neurophysiological findings also suggest that the locus coeruleus may mediate physiological, behavioural and psychological aspects of fear and anxiety. Further, the onset of agoraphobia in some individuals during, or after, major endocrinological/hormonal upheavals (such as with the birth of a baby), implies that such factors may again play a role in the development of the condition. Finally, cardiovascular research suggests that, in some patients, palpitations may be related to cardiac arrythmias[5] – although any direct connection with agoraphobia is by no means clear.

*Chapter 7*

# Further Causal Factors

## i. Precipitating Events

For most agoraphobics, no matter what other predisposing variables play a part, the 'start' of the condition usually follows a period of 'stress', and the experience of a 'panic attack' – though sometimes a series of panic attacks can occur before avoidance behaviour sets in.

Panic attacks are manifested by the sudden onset of intense apprehension, fear of terror, often associated with feelings of impending doom. The most common symptoms experienced during an attack are dyspnoea*; palpitations; chest pain or discomfort; choking or smothering sensations, dizziness, vertigo, or unsteady feelings; feelings of unreality; paresthesias†; hot and cold flushes; sweating; faintness; trembling or shaking; and fear of dying, going crazy, or doing something uncontrolled during the attack. Attacks usually last minutes; more rarely hours'.[1]

A multitude of events can precede the onset of panic attacks and consequent agoraphobic avoidance behaviour. Those most frequently reported as the 'precipitating causes' often involve some emotionally stressful occurrence, or change, in the individual's life. For example, events such as serious illness, bereavement, conflict or stress (at home or at work), leaving home, engagement, marriage, pregnancy or an unpleasant scene in public are common precursors of the condition. Shafar found in her 1976 study of 90 phobics (68 of whom were agoraphobic), that precipitating factors existed in 75 patients (i.e. in 83 per cent of the sample). Of these patients, 57 per cent had relationship problems which constituted the most significant factor at onset (in-

---

* Dyspnoea: difficult or laboured breathing.
† Paresthesia: an abnormal sensation of prickling, tingling, or itching of the skin.

cluding 12 per cent with unhappy childhoods); while, for another 11 per cent, bereavements occurring within five years prior to the onset of symptons were important in precipitating the condition. For the remaining 32 per cent, ten other factors played an important part including: pregnancy and childbirth; separation from a key figure other than by bereavement; change of abode; organic illness or insecurity in employment; accident or assault; psychiatric illness; guilt regarding illicit sex; and guilt regarding abortion.

While the initial attack often takes place suddenly in one great burst, seeming to appear spontaneously 'out of the blue', in some cases the onset is more gradual and the individual recalls the panics being preceded by general feelings of tenseness, nervousness and dizziness. Most sufferers are able to recall vividly the experience and circumstances surrounding their first panic attack; and the occasion is later recalled as having been a pivotal event in their lives. In some cases the initial attacks have even occurred during sleep.

The specific nature of the precipitant has little effect on the subsequent course of the disorder for, once the cycle of panic begins, it develops a self-perpetuating course independent of its original antecedents. Following the first attack, patients experience anxiety in the same or similar situations, but other situations then become associated with fear through generalization from the earlier ones. Subsequent attacks may involve fear that panic will occur in such situations and that the person will be disabled (e.g. by having a heart attack or fainting, or by losing control in some other way). Avoidance behaviour then sets in, as a consequence of these noxious feelings and thoughts, and the individual's behaviour becomes progressively more inhibited.

Marks, in his 1969 book, concludes that many cases of agoraphobia are short-lived. However, phobias which have persisted for a year or more are unlikely to remit over the next several years if untreated – although partial remission can occur. Clinical impressions suggest that agoraphobic symptoms, and the avoidance behaviour that goes with them, are less likely to show improvement over time than other anxiety states.

## ii. Maintaining Factors

Some of the many factors which operate to maintain the agoraphobic's avoidance of situations through fear of panic are outlined below.

COGNITIVE FACTORS*

The way in which patients view their own experiences of anxiety and panic is very important to the maintenance of the condition. Data with respect to the role of feelings and thoughts in determining anxiety are inconclusive, but for some individuals 'fear-inducing self-instructions' and similar imaginings precede the experience of fear. Indeed, some theorists argue that phobic patients have a tendency to think irrationally, and that these irrational beliefs and 'negative self talk' may produce their own characteristically distressing emotions. 'Fear of panic' is an example of this. If sufferers believe that panic will result in a heart attack (because of the palpitations), or fainting (because of hyperventilation and difficulty in breathing), then of course they will fear a panic. In all likelihood, such beliefs will precipitate the very thing the agoraphobic hopes to avoid (i.e. the panic), and the negative and counterproductive thoughts are thus a large part of the problem.

Mathews *et al* in their 1981 book argue that another important feature of agoraphobics' attitudes is an inability to make accurate connections between their emotions and the events that cause them. Thus, their failure to recognize that the anxieties they experience are a consequence of conflict or stress in their lives† may lead them to misinterpret their feelings – so causing them, for example, to believe a panic attack is a sign of impending death or disease. Such debilitating thoughts (e.g. that they will experience panic or collapse and be ridiculed in public places), maintain the avoidance of potentially stressful situations – so preventing resolution of the conflict which may have caused the feelings in the first place.

AVOIDANCE BEHAVIOUR

It is evident that agoraphobics tend to avoid situations where they think they will be engulfed by panic. In doing so they incubate the fear, and maintain the conviction that they will be harmed by the event and the panic which may ensue from it. This in turn leads to further avoidance, so undermining confidence even more and increasing the likelihood of additional panics.

---

* The ways in which a person may think about his or her situation.
† e.g. an argument with their husband or other triggering pressures.

LACK OF ASSERTIVENESS

Many agoraphobics (some of whom are generally fearful and dependent people), are unable to stand up for their rights or even to state clearly what they think. Indeed, research suggests that agoraphobic individuals report a great deal of difficulty in expressing anger or negative feelings towards others, particularly towards family members.[2] This accords with my own experience with clients, many of whom have had great difficulty in asserting themselves. The bottled-up feelings (frequently of aggression and resentment), in turn maintain a high level of tension and arousal, and so contribute further to agoraphobic tendencies.

SECONDARY GAIN FROM THE SYMPTOMS

Some individuals, whether consciously or unconsciously, can obtain benefit from their condition. This may be as simple as getting another member of the family to do the shopping; it may enable avoidance of testing oneself out in the work force if one is unconfident; or it may be a means of resolving marital problems. Remaining dependent on a husband, for example, and enforcing devotion from him because one is 'ill', may enable the patient to avoid some of the difficulties which exist in the relationship. Shafar in her 1976 study, found that psychological gain operated with 70 per cent of her patients, there being no significant differences in this respect between different types of phobias.* Any such condition then becomes more difficult to relinquish and recover from.

## iii. Factors Contributing to and Related to the Intensity of the Symptoms

As mentioned previously, physiological arousal arising from any source (be it, for example, exercise, allergies, caffeine or sweating) is often a cue for panic, even in the absence of environmental stress. Thus Marks and Herst (1970) found that 35 per cent of the 1,200 agoraphobics they surveyed believed that hot weather exacerbated

---

* Sixty-eight out of Shafer's ninety patients were agoraphobic, the remainder exhibiting social or other more specific phobias. There seemed to be no difference in the extent of psychological gain across these three types.

their symptoms. Coffee, and sometimes cigarette smoking, may do likewise; and withdrawal symptoms from drugs and cigarettes can frequently elicit panics. Even thoughts and feelings alone are often sufficient to induce a panic attack; and, indeed, anticipatory anxiety about panic can become a self-fulfilling prophecy. Stressful conditions (e.g. arguments, hurrying, etc.), or the perception of threat, can also induce hyperactivity in the autonomic nervous system. These internal sensations then become cues for people who fear panics, so producing anxiety responses and perceptions of threat – and ultimately panic itself.

## Conclusion

As was discussed at the end of Chapter 2, it appears that multiple factors may interact in determining agoraphobic conditions. *Predisposing* factors include numerous psychosocial and biological variables, which can affect the way in which the individual responds to, and copes with, stress. *Precipitating* factors may be specific to individual sufferers, but they all seem to reflect a common element of stress and the occurrence of panic at some point. Finally, *maintaining* factors include the ways in which the condition becomes self-perpetuating as a result of the individual's fear of her/his own anxiety symptoms – these include avoidance of situations, thereby perpetuating the fear of them; lack of assertiveness, leading to further accumulated tension; and possible secondary gain.

Each individual reflects a unique combination of these factors, manifesting some of the above determinants and not others. A definitive theory of causation is not possible, nor is it desirable, for to focus on unique elements in an individual's psychological make-up is often an essential element in the treatment of patients. Nevertheless, broad trends emerge. There are factors which are common to most individuals suffering from agoraphobia (e.g. fear of the panic or a tendency to avoid stressful situations, etc.); and these various factors may be susceptible to treatment in common ways. However, additional attention should be paid to individualized characteristics, if each person's unique reasons for developing the complaint (and their ways of coping afterwards), are to be understood. Above all, there must be great flexibility in the assessment and treatment of each individual's condition.

## Part III

# Treatment

The following section of the book is intended to serve as a self-help manual for all those wishing to tackle their symptoms directly. As mentioned at the end of the Preface and in Chapter 2, Parts I and III can be read in conjunction with one another to provide information about agoraphobia, its treatment, and how best you can get over it yourself. Part II deals with its origins in greater theoretical detail. For those of you who have read Part II, there may be some repetition in Part III, as the causes are summarized and recapitulated for those moving straight on from Part I.

## Chapter 8

# Explanation and Understanding

## How Does it Begin?

Ross was twenty-six when he referred himself for treatment. He had had the problem for five years and described it as follows:

> I believe I have a phobia about being in closed rooms. I panic and sweat and am scared that others will notice. It's not only inside. I find I get the same reaction when I go out to a new restaurant, meet new people, and go to job interviews. Even in a cinema I break out into a cold sweat . . . It started about five years ago. I first experienced it at work during my training to be a hotel manager. I was working in the banquet department of our main hotel. I was in the office doing the accounting and I had other things to do as well. Suddenly a blast of panic swept over me and I started to sweat profusely. I thought: 'I have to get away, and felt absolutely ghastly. I didn't feel comfortable at all. Since then, it's been like the chicken and egg. I lose confidence because I fear I'm going to sweat, and lo and behold the panic hits and I do sweat. It strikes usually when I'm in a business situation, but it can happen in other situations. I've started to avoid things, and it's really affected me badly. Last summer I had the opportunity to work in a top notch hotel in France during summer, but I avoided it and stayed in London because I felt safer in familiar surroundings . . .

Agoraphobia usually starts with a panic reaction which seems to come 'out of the blue'. The experience is so unpleasant and frightening that people begin to fear its recurrence, as Ross did. Apprehension about it happening again (known as 'anticipatory anxiety') can often precipitate the very thing feared. The same feelings of panic can arise merely by thinking about them. People then begin to avoid the situation where the panic first occurred, be it in a shop, on a tram, train, or subway. Through a process of generalization, avoidance of other situations develops. Movement becomes more and more curtailed. Ross, for example, began to avoid any situation in which he felt he might be trapped. The avoidance was motivated by fear that the feelings of panic would re-emerge, causing something disastrous to happen before escape was possible. For him, the fear was that he would be embarrassingly soaked in sweat. For others, the fear is more severe and consists of fear of dying, fainting or collapsing. Frequently, the disastrous outcome is not clearly envisaged.

The condition varies in severity. In some people, the pattern of avoidance does not develop to any great degree and to cope they merely grit their teeth and ride through the panic without curtailing their activities. This results in perpetual exhaustion, as everyday activity is overlaid by continual, wearing anxiety. For others, avoidance allows them to remain relatively panic-free. Their lifestyle becomes restricted and they become bored, frustrated and depressed. However, this way of coping can keep panic and anxiety to a minimum. With some, both panic and avoidance become a part of everyday life. Not only is their activity curtailed, but even at home there is an overlay of continual exhaustion, anxiety and tension. Sometimes, and perhaps most depressingly, panic attacks begin to occur at home.

## Tackling the Problem

If the above outline rings true and fits your own condition, then the question arises: how can this be tackled?

First and foremost, it is important to ACCEPT that you have a problem. Unless there is an acceptance of the condition, then your way of coping may be counterproductive. For example, someone who stoically grits their teeth and rides through panic may be contributing to its intensity. The 'pull-up-your-socks', 'grin-and-bear-it' attitude may in fact worsen the condition. Instead of learning to cope with the panic and understanding what may have caused it in the first place, denial of the problem can merely exacerbate it. So, ACCEPTANCE OF THE CONDITION is a first and vital step.

It is also important to begin to UNDERSTAND how the condition arises. I find that a useful way of explaining the condition to

## Fig. 2 The Development of Agoraphobia

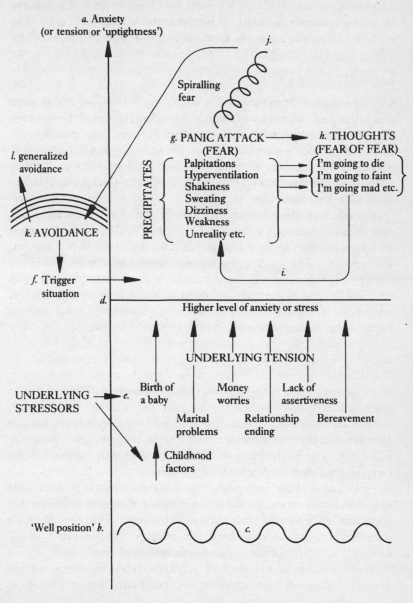

agoraphobic patients is through the use of a diagram. (Refer to Fig. 2.) Many of them say 'Aha! that is exactly how it is', as we go through the steps in the diagram, so it may be useful to follow it through. It must be read like a flow chart, moving from point *a.* to *b.* to *c.* and so on.

EXPLANATION OF FIG. 2

i. If we visualize the vertical arrow *a.* as anxiety (tension, physiological arousal, or just 'general uptightness'), it is useful to speculate where we fall on that continuum when we feel relaxed and calm. Most people locate their 'well position' somewhere low on the scale, for example at point *b.* This of course fluctuates from day to day, according to whether there are traffic jams, whether or not you've had a good night's sleep, etc. (Refer to point *c.* on the diagram.)

ii. Now, what seems to happen in the development of agoraphobia is that sufferers develop a higher level of general anxiety (located at point *d.*) than when they are well. This usually follows a period of prolonged or sudden stress. The sources of stress vary from individual to individual. (Refer to point *e.* on the diagram, to see how underlying stressors contribute to the anxiety level.) For some women, the higher level of anxiety may occur after the birth of a baby. (This may be due both to hormonal shifts and stresses induced by lifestyle changes.) For other people it may occur after prolonged marital difficulties, money worries, the stress of study and exams, the ending of a relationship, moving house, illness, a bereavement, etc. Diffuse anxiety may be a reflection of any or all of these stresses. For some (but not all) patients, earlier life stresses (such as an unhappy childhood or the early loss of an important figure), seem to contribute to this overall picture of bottled-up tension. Lack of assertiveness also characterizes many people with this condition. An inability to express feelings, wishes and desires may be one of the contributing factors to the underlying tension.

iii. The onset of the first panic attack occurs in most patients only after cumulative stress has led to a high level of anxiety. Some people are not aware of this diffuse anxiety until their first panic precipitates it into their awareness. An event or situation occurs (refer to *f.* in the diagram) which is like the 'straw that breaks the camel's back'. It may be running for a crowded bus on a hot day, entering a busy supermarket, finding a seat in a packed theatre or simply having a cup of coffee after a pressured morning. It is as if the underlying tension has been tipped over into something entirely different, resulting in the first panic attack (refer to *g.* in the diagram). This may consist of palpitations (heart pounding), hyperventilation (difficulty in getting your breath), shaky (or 'jelly') legs and muscles, sweatiness, hot and cold flushes, pins and needles, numbness, blurred vision and feelings of weakness, dizziness and unreality.

iv. These symptoms are those of a normal fear response, but they occur in a situation which is not normally fearful. I explain the feelings to my patients as follows:

Imagine that a bomb suddenly dropped out there in the courtyard [I have a courtyard outside my office]. We would immediately feel terrified. Adrenaline would start pumping round our bodies, preparing us with the 'fight/flight response' to flee. Automatically, we would breathe more deeply to get further oxygen into our systems, our hearts would pump more quickly to circulate it effectively, our muscles would be activated, ready to run. Now what seems to happen in the development of agoraphobia, is that the underlying tension caused by stress, lowers your fear threshold. A relatively small, non-fearful stimulus can trigger off a full-blown fear response, appropriate to a bomb. But because there is no bomb around (merely a bus, or a supermarket) you begin to have thoughts about what is happening to you. (Refer to *h.* in the diagram.) You think: 'Heavens! I'm having a heart attack! I'm going to die!', thereby misinterpreting the palpitations. You think: 'I can't get my breath! I'm going to faint.' You also think: 'I don't know what's happening to me. It feels as if I'm going mad!'

People have different thoughts about the feelings, but one thing is common to them all. The thoughts are anxiety-provoking in their own right and make the panic worse. (Refer to *i.*) The panic then escalates to the point where you are experiencing possibly more fear than you would in the face of a bomb. (Refer to *j.* for a feedback loop where the thoughts make the panic worse.) The feeling is so excruciating that you begin to avoid the situation in which the first panic occurred. (Refer to *k*). The avoidance then generalizes to similar situations, through fear of the feelings occurring again. For example, if the panic occurred on a train you say: 'A tram is like a train, so I won't go on a tram. A bus is like a tram, so I won't go on a bus. A shop queue is like a bus, because you're trapped there and can't get out, so I won't go there . . .' etc, etc.

A pattern of generalization occurs in which you begin to avoid more and more situations (refer to *l*.). Some people get to the point where they only feel safe at home; while others find that the feelings encroach there as well.

In essence, what happens is that underlying tension leads up to the first *panic attack* which occurs seemingly 'out of the blue'. This produces *frightening thoughts* about what is happening and where it might lead. These result in a *worsening of the panic* and consequent *avoidance* of situations where you fear the panic might occur.

In some individuals, the series of events described in Fig. 2 may occur very rapidly. In others, it may take longer, sometimes even years. The following chapter outlines how treatment begins.

## Chapter 9

# Steps in Treatment: An Outline

The aim of treatment is to enable you to:

1. cope with panic without avoiding it,
2. resolve the underlying issues which have produced the cumulative tension in the first place,
3. tackle the situations that you have been avoiding,
4. develop greater confidence and self-esteem, and help you to cope better with stresses in the future.

There are several main steps to be taken in the treatment of panic and agoraphobia, in addition to the acceptance and understanding of the condition as outlined in the previous chapter. These steps are illustrated in Fig. 3.

## i. Learning to Relax

There are two main reasons for learning to relax. Firstly, if you practise regularly (preferably at least once a day accompanied by a tape), you will find that it lowers your general tension level (refer to point *a.* in Fig. 3). This will make you less prone to panic, as the underlying tension lessens.

Secondly, relaxation training will provide you with strategies to deal with the panic (refer to point *b.*). If you are relaxed: taking long deep breaths, lowering your hunched-up shoulders, unclenching your fists, ·you will find it hard to panic. Panic and relaxation are incompatible responses and one will help to inhibit the other. It takes a long time and a lot of practice to use relaxation in this way; many people say the panic engulfs them so quickly that it is impossible to implement the procedures early enough. However, with practice, relaxation can be used to catch a panic before it spirals to a level where flight feels necessary.

## Fig. 3 Components of Treatment

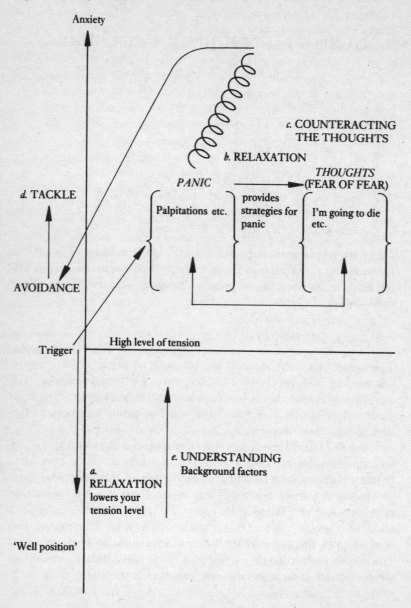

Some researchers suggest that relaxation does not provide effective treatment for agoraphobia, but their results remain questionable on several grounds. First, they studied groups of people with the condition and their findings reflect an average of the individuals' responses. The overall conclusion that relaxation was ineffective may therefore reflect both the responses of individuals who found it helpful and those who did not. Averages would 'iron out' these differences. Also, relaxation was the only technique used. The finding that it was ineffective is therefore not surprising. It needs to be practised in conjunction with other methods for it to be fully effective in counteracting panic.

Work with my own patients suggests that individuals vary in their response to relaxation. Many have found it extremely useful both as a 'general calmer', and as a strategy for dealing directly with panic. Others have found it less helpful and have relied more heavily on other procedures for tackling the problem.

People find that some techniques work well for them, while others work less well or not at all. This is not a reason for despair, merely an indication that different techniques are appropriate to different individuals. Treatment is like a shopping expedition that you must persist in. Some things suit, and some do not; so the search needs to continue until the right techniques are found.

With regard to relaxation, although the majority find it of direct benefit, approximately 5–10 per cent of people experience a phenomenon known as 'relaxation-induced-anxiety'. As they begin to practise the techniques for the first time, these people notice a growing sense of tension, and sometimes panic or depression; indeed some even find tears spring to their eyes, and then worry that they should be reacting in this way. A few individuals use this as a pretext for avoiding the relaxation techniques but, in response to this, I encourage them to persist and to try to ride through this initial response to the exercises.

For those people who have been over-active (perhaps using their activity as a defence against underlying feelings), slowing down and relaxing can be distressing and aversive. Relaxation can be a new state to them and, because of its novelty, anxiety-provoking. It is important to work through this phase and to persist with the exercises despite their difficulty; it may be that the over-activity is one of the factors contributing to tension and panic and it therefore needs to be tackled directly.

(For a detailed outline of Relaxation Procedures, refer to Chapter 10.)

## ii Counteracting the Thoughts

This step is best done in parallel with learning to relax, and the two techniques need to work together to be fully effective. (Refer to Fig. 3 point *c*.)

The thoughts regarding panic are perhaps the strongest part in the chain leading from panic to avoidance and agoraphobia. As we have seen, agoraphobics can misinterpret their feelings and think that they are having a heart attack, that they are going to die, faint, or lose control in a socially embarrassing way. Claire Weekes refers to this as the 'fear of fear', and it is one form of 'anticipatory anxiety'. Patients anticipate they will panic in certain situations and frequently this is enough to cause it. It is largely this fear of panic that keeps their anxiety alive. They fear what 'will' happen to them 'if' they panic.

This 'what if' mentality (an apprehension about the future), needs to be changed. The feelings of panic do not result in the envisaged consequences, and though I have seen more than 200 people with the condition, in not one of them have their worst fears been realized.

On the other hand, for some patients the worst fears of others would offer them a blessed relief. Those who fear going mad or dying sometimes say they wish they could faint (a consequence which others fear so much). In this case, a necessary component of treatment is for the patient to learn that such thoughts are unfounded, unrealistic and irrational. People don't die from panic attacks – nor have any of those affected by panics whom I have seen, or heard of, gone mad or lost control in a totally irrecoverable manner in the situation in which they have feared doing so.

The anticipation of 'the worst' needs to be tackled and 'gathered back', so that you begin to observe what is really happening in your body, not what you think might happen. For example, take your pulse. It will probably be racing much faster than usual if you are feeling panicky; but so it would if you had just been for a run or a swim. A racing pulse does not mean that you are about to drop dead of a heart attack. Panic feels terrible, but it does not result in anything worse than panic. The automatic thoughts about panic are the problem, like a stuck record playing over and over with the groove getting deeper and deeper. In Chapter 10, various strategies are outlined in order to help you deal with these thoughts directly.

## iii Tackling Things at Your Own Pace

Agoraphobia does not get better unless you begin to tackle the situations you have been avoiding (refer to point *d.* in Fig. 3). Going back to places where you have had the panic, and learning to cope with the feelings, is a crucial part of treatment. Even Freud acknowledged the importance of encouraging phobic patients to tackle their anxiety directly, rather than just talking about it. Simply developing insight into it is not enough. He advised therapists that:

> One can hardly ever master a phobia if one waits till the patient lets the analyst influence him to give it up . . . One succeeds only when one can induce them through the influence of the analysis to . . . go about alone and to struggle with their anxiety while they make the attempt.[1]

Thus, learning to relax and face anxiety in feared situations is crucial. Claire Weekes, in her excellent book *Agoraphobia: Simple Effective Treatment*, outlines four concepts useful in coping with panic. These are: facing, accepting, floating and letting time pass; and she details the four concepts as follows:

> FACE the feelings. Do not run away from them or try to avoid them by distraction. To try to switch the panic off, and to avoid its coming, brings no permanent cure. Try to confront the feelings directly without avoidance.
> ACCEPT the feelings. Try not to fight against them or tense yourself even further to keep the feelings at bay. True acceptance means welcoming panic as an opportunity to practise coping with it. [She maintains that the best way to remember panic is trying hard to forget it!]
> FLOAT. Go with the feelings. Try to go with them and not to tense against them. (This is where relaxation can help.) Try to let yourself go slack and float past the obstructive thoughts (the 'fear of fear') that undermine your confidence. Go along with the feelings, as if floating on the sea.
> LET TIME PASS. Impatience increases tension and anxiety, so try not to be impatient with time or worry that the cure is slow. It may

be that improvement takes a long time, since the symptoms have been with you for a long time. There is no instant cure or magical pill for the problem, so take it at its own pace and try not to push it.

What Claire Weekes highlights here is that getting better is not just a matter of getting used to the situations one is avoiding. For lasting recovery, you need to learn to cope with the symptoms themselves, the feelings of panic and tension, and not just the places you have purposely avoided for months or years.

Some people find that the tendency to panic decreases considerably after talking through their problem and they then find they don't panic when they tackle anxiety-producing situations. Others find that avoidance has kept them anxiety-free, and anxiety and panic do reemerge when they face such situations again. These feelings have to be confronted and worked through: using relaxation, counteracting the thoughts and using the four concepts described above.

Some therapists use what is known as the 'flooding' approach with their clients. This means that they accompany the person to the situation he or she fears most (e.g. the tube train) and stay with them until their anxiety subsides. This enables the person to be confronted with the most feared situation and so prove that nothing disastrous will happen as a result of the panic. I tend not to use this approach, although I did in the initial stages of treatment of some of my patients. When I first graduated, the research literature suggested that flooding was the most effective technique. So I spent many wearisome hours in the London Underground with doubly weary patients, going round and round the Circle Line, explaining panic and reassuring them if they felt tense and anxious. One patient returned to me after a twelve-month break from treatment saying that, whilst she had developed an aversion to this mode of therapy, we had a good enough relationship to continue working together, using an alternative approach. From this, and from reports of patients who referred themselves to me after having similar treatment, I concluded that flooding treatment may even cause clients to develop a phobia about their therapist! For some, it is appropriate. For others, going into feared situations needs to occur at a more gradual rate.

I prefer to help people tackle things at their own pace. Although this sometimes means that I do actually accompany them into the feared situations, on the whole, I ask patients to begin tackling things, no matter how small, on their own. Then they gradually build up their achievements slowly, at their own pace, and under their own control. This approach is referred to as 'desensitization' and contrasts with the more abrupt technique of 'flooding'. Either approach can work, but the pace of improvement depends on the person and the speed at which they are prepared to tackle things.

Some patients are helped by relaxing and imagining the feared situations before tackling them in the real world. Eventually, however, '*in vivo* desensitization' is necessary – i.e. facing things in reality (rather than in imagination) in an increasing order of difficulty. Housebound people need to use exactly the same procedures. However, if you are housebound, it is useful, and frequently necessary, to have someone help you tackle going into the outside world again. It is best if your helper is well versed in the techniques of coping with panic; if possible, it may be worth enlisting the aid of a therapist who undertakes home visits. Further techniques which have been developed to help patients tackle panic-producing situations are discussed in the next chapter.

## iv. Developing Insight into Underlying Causes

According to Iris G. Fodor in her article 'The Phobic Syndrome in Women', there are two major approaches to the treatment of agoraphobia: the psychoanalytical and the behavioural. Each evolved from two divergent theoretical backgrounds and they focus on different things. One emphasizes insight and understanding as the way to get better; the other emphasizes the learning of new non-avoidance behaviours, thereby changing the phobic symptoms directly. Neither approach seems to incorporate elements of the other.

During nine years of working with agoraphobia and the fear of panic, I have come to recognize that it is important to work on both levels. Many patients who have referred themselves to me for help have already tried the analytic approach. For example, Katherine (introduced in Chapter 1), had been to an analytic therapist for five years during the 27-year duration of her problem. There had been little or no symptom relief during that time, although she had been helped in other areas of her life. John, a young man of twenty-seven, whose problems of panic and avoidance had lasted for six years before

I saw him, had been to both a psychiatrist and an analytically-oriented psychologist for considerable periods. His therapy with the psychologist seemed to have given him some insight into his family structure and childhood; however, the symptoms had not budged.

Both of these patients illustrate a motto of mine that 'you can understand the causes until the cows come home, but this will not give you strategies to cope with the panic'. It may be (although this is rarely the case), that the underlying difficulties have remitted or subsided, but the symptoms remain because they have become largely autonomous and self-perpetuating. If people avoid things through fear of panic which they think will cause something disastrous to happen, then the avoidance incubates the fear and keeps it alive. They never actually prove to themselves that they can cope, and that their worst fears will not eventuate, until they have finally tackled the dreaded situations.

On the other hand, however, a purely behavioural approach is frequently inadequate, too. Jenny (introduced in Chapter 3) had seen a clinical psychologist and a psychiatrist and had been to a highly thought of one-week residential behavioural programme for agoraphobics. None of these treatments had removed the symptoms permanently.

In some patients, whilst the behavioural emphasis on dealing with the symptoms is necessary, it is totally insufficient for coping with the problem. Mary (forty-three years old) had been agoraphobic for eighteen months when I saw her, after she had developed panic and avoidance to the degree of being almost totally housebound. In addition to understanding her symptoms, learning to relax, and beginning to tackle things gradually, it was essential for her to talk about underlying issues. Her youngest brother had become schizophrenic in his early teens, when she was sixteen, and he had been in and out of hospital for years until he died in hospital at the age of thirty-four. No one knew exactly how he had died. Her mother had been unable to come to terms with his illness, and had been in and out of hospital herself during the twenty-year period. Upon his death, Mary's mother felt that her house was haunted by his ghost, so she came to live with Mary, her husband and three children. They had been planning to move, so they bought a house with a granny flat at the end of a long garden but, after three months, her mother still felt she could not cope, so she moved permanently into an old people's home. Mary's sixteen-year-old son then moved into the flat to gain some independence. He got into 'bad company' (some of his friends were into drugs and petty crime) and they came to visit him there. About a year later, Mary had to go into hospital for a hysterectomy, and during this time her son took an overdose. He survived, but Mary, of course, worried about him and feared that he was becoming like her younger brother. She had her first panic attack one week after coming out of hospital and over the next eighteen months her symptoms had become progressively worse.

Now, for Mary, it was absolutely crucial to talk about these underlying issues. A major part of treatment involved her coming to terms with hidden feelings of resentment both towards her mother and towards her younger sister who had not helped during any of these events. In conjunction with learning to handle and face up to the panic, she had to learn how to be more assertive. Both aspects of treatment were necessary to get her out and about again, and to build up her confidence.

Although many patients' backgrounds do not seem as trying as Mary's, it is nonetheless necessary to understand how their tension has built up in the first place (refer to point *e.* in Fig. 3). Anne (introduced in Chapter 1), developed a high level of tension, as many women do, during that taxing period of having to look after two young children at home; her eldest had just started school and renovations were being carried out on the house when she had her first panic. In looking at her background, however, it became apparent that her problems went back much further. She had always wanted to be a teacher, but had not received good enough Higher School Certificate results to get into the teachers' college of her choice. She therefore undertook secretarial training and then found a job as chief secretary and administrator at a small girls' school. She thoroughly enjoyed this. However, she discovered from a friend's father that she would now be eligible for further tuition at a small teachers' college run by a Church organization. She applied and was accepted, but after a month found the quality of the training so abysmal that she left. However, by then her job had been taken, so she returned to the same school as a temporary assistant in the library until she got married some six months later. She was still angry about these events when she came for treatment eight-and-a-half years later.

It is usually the case that there are difficulties like these which make the emergence of tension in the near or distant past explicable. Each individual's life history indicates how the cumulative tension has arisen and, once this is understood, it is frequently possible to help the patient tackle the symptoms.

So, it is important to understand this in your own situation, and to discuss it with someone who will help you work through it. Some techniques for beginning to piece together the pattern of your life as it has emerged so far will be outlined in the next chapter.

## v. Developing Confidence and Self-Esteem

Rather than seeing the development of confidence and self-esteem as a next step in treatment, it is important to see this as an accompanying by-product of the preceding steps. As you begin to understand things more clearly, as you begin to relax, counteract your negative thoughts and tackle things you have been avoiding, your confidence will grow.

The main emphasis should be on increasing your confidence rather than merely tackling your anxiety. Both involve essentially the same thing, but one is positively formulated: moving on to something new; the other is negatively formulated: getting rid of something old. There are various ways of facilitating this growth in confidence and self-esteem, and these, too, will be discussed in the next chapter.

## Chapter 10

# Tackling the Symptoms Directly

## i. Reading

One important adjunct to all the aspects of therapy mentioned so far is reading about the methods of treatment. There are many helpful books available and the more you read, the more ideas you will have about what will work for you. The following titles are particularly worthwhile. (An introductory self-help book list is also included in Appendix A.)

*For Agoraphobia*
Claire Weekes, *Agoraphobia: Simple Effective Treatment*, Angus & Robertson, 1977
J. Clarke and Wayne Wardman, *Agoraphobia: A Personal and Clinical Account*, Pergamon Press, 1985
A. Mathews, M. Gelder and D. Johnston, *Programmed Practice for Agoraphobia* (2 books for you and your partner), Tavistock Publications, 1981

(It is perhaps best to begin with Claire Weekes' book, although the others also provide many useful ideas.)

*To Counteract the Thoughts*
A good book to start with is:
Wayne Dyer, *Your Erroneous Zones*, Sphere Books, 1977

*For Assertiveness*
M. Smith, *When I Say No I Feel Guilty*, Bantam Books, 1975
H. Fensterheim & J. Baer, *Don't Say Yes When You Want To Say No*, Futura Publications, 1976
Anne Dickson, *A Woman in Your Own Right: Assertiveness and You*, Quartet Books, 1982. (For women obviously.)

All of these books are at least worth dipping into, so try to find them in your local library. If they are not in the catalogue, then get the librarian to order them. Try to buy at least one or two of them, because it helps to have your own 'Self-Help Library' on hand for reference every now and then, if not every day.

## ii. Learning to Relax

As mentioned in the previous chapter, relaxation is useful for two reasons:

 i. It lowers your general tension level.
 ii. It provides you with strategies for dealing with the panic when it occurs.

Two methods of relaxation are outlined below – the first is a long form, and the second a short form. It is useful to put both of these on tape by reading the instructions very slowly into a tape recorder. If you don't want to hear your own voice, get your husband, wife or a friend to do it for you. Alternatively, you could buy a tape ready-made. A list of some of the tapes available is provided in Appendix B at the back of this book.

PROGRESSIVE RELAXATION EXERCISES

These should last for about 20–25 minutes. They teach you how to relax the body entirely, by demonstrating the difference between tensing and relaxing your muscles. The exercises move through the different parts of your body: arms, face, neck, shoulders, chest, stomach, lower back and legs; they focus on breathing (very important) and overall relaxation. Try to do these exercises at least once a day. If you wake up tense, switch on your tape and practise the techniques; this is better than lying in bed worrying, jumping up for a cigarette or charging full-tilt into the day. If you feel tense before you go shopping, do them then; or, if you come home from work exhausted, run through them again. Find a warm, quiet room, and either sit in a comfortable armchair or lie flat on your back on a full-length couch, or even on the floor. At night, you can lie in bed doing the exercises to help you go to sleep.

Make sure that your legs are uncrossed and out-stretched, and that your arms are comfortably by your side. Close your eyes and let yourself relax as much as you can. The exercises will enable you to become less tense until you are, at the end of them, very deeply relaxed:

*Relaxation of arms* (time: 5–6 minutes)

Settle back as comfortably as you can. Let yourself relax to the best of your ability . . .

Now, as you relax like that, clench your right fist, just clench it tighter and tighter, and study the tension as you do so. Keep it clenched and feel the tension in your right fist, hand, forearm . . . and now relax. Let the fingers of your right hand become loose, and observe the contrast in your feelings . . . Now, let yourself go, and try to become more relaxed all over . . . Once more, clench your right fist really tight . . . hold it, and notice the tension again . . . Now let go, relax; your fingers straighten out, and you notice the difference once more . . . Now repeat that with your left fist. Clench your left fist while the rest of your body relaxes; clench that fist tighter and feel the tension . . . and now relax. Again enjoy the contrast . . . Repeat that once more, clench the left fist, tight and tense . . . Now do the opposite of tension, relax and feel the difference. Continue relaxing like that for a while . . . Now, clench both fists, tighter and tighter, both fists tense, forearms tense, study the sensations . . . and relax; straighten out your fingers and feel that relaxation. Continue relaxing your hands and forearms more and more . . . Now bend your elbows and tense your biceps, tense them harder and study the tension feelings . . . All right, straighten out your arms, let them relax and feel the difference again. Let the relaxation develop . . . Once more, tense your biceps; hold the tension and observe it carefully . . . Now, straighten the arms and relax; relax to the best of your ability . . . Each time, pay close attention to your feelings when you tense up and when you relax. Now straighten your arms, reach for the ceiling, straighten them so that you feel most tension in the triceps muscles along the back of your arms; stretch your arms and feel that tension . . . And now relax. Get your arms back into a comfortable position. Let the relaxation proceed on its own. The arms should feel comfortably heavy as you allow them to relax . . . Straighten them. Feel that tension . . . and relax . . . Now let's concentrate on pure relaxation in the arms without any tension. Get your arms comfortable and let them relax further and further. Continue relaxing your arms even further. Even when your arms are soon fully relaxed, try to go that extra bit further, try to achieve deeper and deeper levels of relaxation.

*Relaxation of facial area with neck, shoulders and upper back* (time: 5–6 minutes)

Let all your muscles go loose and heavy. Just settle back quietly and comfortably. Wrinkle up your forehead now; wrinkle it tighter . . . And now stop wrinkling your forehead, relax, and smooth it out. Picture the entire forehead and scalp becoming smoother as the relaxation increases . . . Now frown and crease your brows and study the tension . . . Let go of the tension again. Smooth out the forehead once more . . . Now, close your eyes tighter and tighter . . . feel the tension . . . and relax your eyes. Keep your eyes closed, gently, comfortably, and notice the relaxation . . . Now clench your jaws, bite your teeth together, study the tension throughout the jaws . . . Relax your jaws now. Let your lips part slightly . . . Appreciate the relaxation . . . Now press your tongue hard against the roof of your mouth, look for the tension . . . All right, let your tongue return to a comfortable and relaxed position . . . Now purse your lips, press your lips together tighter and tighter . . . Relax your lips. Note the contrast between tension and relaxation. Feel the relaxation all over your face, all over your forehead and scalp, eyes, jaws, lips, tongue and throat. The relaxation progresses further and further . . . Now attend to your neck muscles. Press your head back as far as it can go and feel the tension in the neck; . . . roll it to the right and feel the tension shift; . . . now roll it to the left . . . Straighten your head and bring it forward, press your chin against your chest . . . Let your head return to a comfortable position, and study the relaxation. Let the relaxation develop . . . Shrug your shoulders, right up. Hold the tension . . . Drop your shoulders and feel the relaxation. Neck, and shoulders relaxed . . . Shrug your shoulders again and move them around. Bring your shoulders up and forward and back. Feel the tension in your shoulders and in your upper back . . . Drop your shoulders once more and relax. Let the relaxation spread deep into the shoulders, right into your back muscles; relax your neck and throat, and your jaws, and other facial areas as the pure relaxation takes over and grows deeper . . . deeper . . . ever . . . deeper.

*Relaxation of chest, stomach and lower back* (time: 5–6 minutes)

Relax your entire body to the best of your ability. Feel that comfortable heaviness which accompanies relaxation. Breathe easily and freely, in and out, just feel that relaxation . . . Now breathe right in and fill your lungs; inhale deeply and hold your breath. Study the tension . . . Now exhale, let the walls of your chest grow loose and push the air out automatically. Continue relaxing and breathe freely and gently. Feel the relaxation and enjoy it . . . With the rest of your body as relaxed as possible, fill your lungs again. Breathe in deeply and hold it again . . . That's fine, breathe out and appreciate the relief. Just breathe normally. Continue relaxing your chest and let the relaxation spread to your back, shoulders, neck and arms. Merely let go . . . and enjoy the relaxation. Now let's pay attention to your abdominal muscles, your stomach area. Tighten your stomach muscles, make your abdomen hard. Notice the tension . . . And relax. Let the muscles loosen and notice the contrast. Once more, press and tighten your stomach muscles. Hold the tension and study it . . . And relax.

Notice the general well-being that comes with relaxing your stomach . . . Now draw your stomach in, pull the muscles right in and feel the tension this way . . . Now relax again. Let your stomach out. Continue breathing normally and easily and feel the gentle massaging action all over your chest and stomach . . . Now pull your stomach in again and hold the tension . . . Now push out and tense like that; hold the tension . . . once more pull in and feel the tension . . . Now relax your stomach fully. Let the tension dissolve as the relaxation grows deeper. Each time you breathe out, notice the rhythmic relaxation both in your lungs and in your stomach. Notice thereby how your chest and your stomach relax more and more . . . Try and let go of all contractions anywhere in your body . . . Now direct your attention to your lower back. Arch up your back, make your lower back quite hollow and feel the tension along your spine . . . and settle down comfortably again relaxing the lower back . . . Just arch your back up and feel the tension as you do so. Try to keep the rest of your body as relaxed as possible. Try to localize the tension throughout your lower back area . . . Relax once more, relaxing further and further. Relax your lower back, relax your upper back, spread the relaxation to your stomach, chest, shoulders, arms and facial area. These parts relaxing further and further and further and ever deeper . . .

*Relaxation of hips, thighs and calves followed by complete relaxation* (time: 5–6 minutes)

Let go of all tensions and relax . . . Now flex your buttocks and thighs. Flex your thighs by pressing down your heels as hard as you can . . . Relax, and note the difference . . . Straighten your knees and flex your thigh muscles again. Hold the tension . . . Relax your hips and thighs. Allow the relaxation to proceed on its own . . . Press your feet and toes downwards, away from your face, so that your calf muscles become tense. Study that tension . . . Relax your feet and calves . . . This time, bend your feet towards your face so that you feel tension along your shins. Bring your toes right up . . . Relax again. Keep relaxing for a while. Now let yourself relax further all over. Relax your feet, ankles, calves and shins, knees, thighs, buttocks and hips. Feel the heaviness of your lower body as you relax still further . . . Now spread the relaxation to your stomach, waist, lower back. Let go more and more. Feel that relaxation all over. Let it proceed to your upper back, chest, shoulders and arms, and right to the tips of your fingers. Keep relaxing more and more deeply. Make sure that no tension has crept into your throat; relax your neck and your jaws and all your facial muscles. Keep relaxing your whole body like that for a while. Let yourself relax. Now you can become twice as relaxed as you are, merely by taking in a really deep breath and slowly exhaling. With your eyes closed so that you become less aware of objects and movements around you and thus prevent any surface tensions from developing, breathe in deeply and feel yourself becoming heavier. Take in a long breath and let it out very slowly . . . Feel how heavy and relaxed you have become.

In a state of perfect relaxation you should feel unwilling to move a single muscle in your body. Think about the effort that would be required to raise your right arm. As you think about raising your right arm, see if you can notice any tensions that might have crept into your shoulder and your arm . . . Now you decide not to lift the arm but to continue relaxing. Observe the relief and the disappearance of the tension. Just carry on relaxing like that. . . . When you wish to get up, count backwards from four to one. You should then feel fine and refreshed, wide awake and calm.

## AUTOGENIC RELAXATION METHOD [1]

This short form should last for about 5–10 minutes and is useful if you haven't much time. For example, when you need to go out in about 10 minutes or when you are at work and face a difficult meeting in 15 minutes. It is also useful because, unlike the previous exercises, you can do it wherever you are without being noticed. To do these exercises, settle back in your chair, and make yourself as comfortable as you can. Uncross your legs and drop your arms down by your side or on to the arms of the chair. Close your eyes, if the situation allows, and visualize the following statements in a slow and relaxed fashion. (Play the tape when and if possible.)

*Phase 1*
My right arm is heavy (Pause)
My right arm is very heavy (Pause)

My left arm is heavy (Pause)
My left arm is very heavy (Pause)

Both arms are heavy (Pause)
Both arms are very heavy (Pause)

My right leg is heavy (Pause)
My right leg is very heavy (Pause)

My left leg is heavy (Pause)
My left leg is very heavy (Pause)

Both legs are heavy (Pause)
Both legs are very heavy (Pause)

*Phase 2*
My right arm is warm (Pause)
My right arm is very warm (Pause)

My left arm is warm (Pause)
My left arm is very warm (Pause)

Both arms are warm (Pause)
Both arms are very warm (Pause)

My right leg is warm (Pause)
My right leg is very warm (Pause)

My left leg is warm (Pause)
My left leg is very warm (Pause)

Both legs are warm (Pause)
Both legs are very warm (Pause)

*Phase 3*
My neck and shoulders are heavy (Pause)
My neck and shoulders are very heavy (Pause)

My body breathes me (Take a deep breath)
(Repeat) My body breathes me (Pause) . . . and RELAX

Open your eyes and sit for a moment or so, feeling relaxed. Then get up and calmly proceed with your next activity.

Try to keep a diary, to indicate how frequently you practise relaxation. A useful format for this will be discussed in the section on 'Tackling Things' later in this chapter.

### iii. Replacing the Negative Thoughts

As mentioned previously, the deeply ingrained thoughts about panic are a major part of the problem. These have usually been learnt on the basis of 'one trial learning'; the first experience of panic is often so aversive that the person's initial interpretation of what is happening to them ('I'm having a heart attack', 'I'm going to collapse', 'I'm going mad', etc), becomes clamped into their mind as the only explanation. This then motivates their attempts to avoid having such feelings again.

The thoughts are automatic, irrational and seemingly resistant to reasoning; it feels as if these things will occur, and no amount of reasoning can change those feelings – at least initially. With hard work, however, the thoughts themselves can be changed, thereby preventing them from adding to the panic. It is like moving the needle on a stuck record. Techniques are needed to stop the obsessive thoughts from going round and round in one's head.

One very useful strategy is learning the ten rules for coping with panic as outlined by Mathews, Gelder and Johnston in their *Programmed Practice for Agoraphobia* (1981). It is worthwhile having these 'Ten Golden Rules' written out on several sheets of paper, so that you can carry one around with you all the time; in your handbag or in your pocket. Stick one up, for example, on your bathroom or dressing-table mirror to help you relearn the list each day. When panicky feelings emerge, take the list out and read it. The rules are as follows:

1. Remember that the feelings are nothing more than an exaggeration of normal bodily reactions to stress.
2. They are not in the least harmful or dangerous – just unpleasant. Nothing worse will happen.
3. Stop adding to panic with frightening thoughts about what will happen and where it might lead.
4. Notice what is really happening in your body right now, not what you fear might happen.
5. Wait, and give the fear time to pass. Do not fight it or run away from it. Just accept it.
6. Notice that once you stop adding to it with frightening thoughts, the fear starts to fade by itself.
7. Remember that the whole point of practising is to learn how to cope with fear – without avoiding it. So this is an opportunity to make progress.
8. Think about the progress you have made so far, despite all the difficulties. Think how pleased you will be when you succeed this time.
9. When you begin to feel better, look around and start to plan what to do next.
10. When you are ready, start off in an easy, relaxed way. There is no need for effort or hurry.

Read the rules in full, and have a shortened form available on another list, or on the back of the longer list. Then, try to remember the longer list, using only the short one as a reminder, as follows:

1. These feelings are normal bodily reactions.
2. They are not harmful.
3. Do not add frightening thoughts.
4. Describe what is happening now.
5. Wait for fear to pass.
6. Notice when it fades.
7. This is an opportunity for progress.
8. Think of what you have done.
9. Plan what to do next.
10. Then start off slower.

Many patients say to me that the last thing in the world they think of doing, or feel inclined to do when on the verge of panic, is to take out a long list of rules and peruse them; the panic engulfs them so quickly that they feel powerless to do anything much except freeze or flee. Nonetheless, with practice, these new thoughts begin to breach the defences of the old negative thoughts. Indeed, some patients read through the list several times in preparation for anxiety-provoking events and find that it helps them stay calm. Others find it a comfort to know that the list is present in their handbag when they're on a bus, even if they don't take it out.

Another useful method of overcoming the negative thoughts and counteracting the panic is to work out a number of 'Coping Statements' chosen by yourself. These may be rehearsed over and over, or written on a sheet to be kept in your pocket, and used in situations where you fear panic.

I recently saw a courageous 71-year-old woman called Sarah, who had had debilitating panic attacks after she had retired from her job ten years previously. It had got to the point where she could no longer get out of the car when her husband took her shopping, as she had been overwhelmed by a very bad panic in the supermarket during an earlier trip. She also found it impossible to go out of her house unaccompanied. When she came back to see me, a week after her first visit, she had practised relaxation twice every day. She had driven to the supermarket with her husband and had walked tentatively into the store on her own, saying to herself as she went: *'Relax. Slow down. These feelings will not get the better of me. Relax. Slow down.'*

She had walked back to the car slowly and deliberately; though previously she had rushed back as fast as she could, saying to her husband on getting into the car: 'Give me my puffer! Give me my puffer!' (She gets emphesema and uses an inhaler when her breathing becomes difficult.) On this occasion, however, she stood outside the car leaning against the bonnet. When her husband opened the window and said, 'Perhaps you should get in. It's cold. Don't you want your puffer?', she said, 'No', and stood a bit longer. She then got in without using the inhaler.

Sarah had also attempted each day to walk slowly down the garden path to the front gate; and to stand on the verandah before going in for about 5–10 minutes – just watching the world go by. Each day, it became a little easier as she said to herself: 'You did it yesterday. The panic didn't come. Relax . . . Slow down . . . Feel calm . . . You're doing all right. You're getting better . . . Don't let the panic get hold of you . . .' Thus, she was able to use these coping self statements, or internal commentaries, to help herself feel stronger, and more res-ilient. Later in therapy, she developed a statement which turned out to be of great benefit to her when facing any fearful situation. She would say: 'Don't be silly! It's not a tiger . . . it's a cat!' This helped her to diminish the extent of her fear and she found herself able to cope again.

Many people, once they have started to tackle the panic, begin, like Sarah, to voice their feelings internally. Sometimes they may get very angry with the panic and fulminate against it; and, if such behaviour doesn't result in them getting even more tense, it can help!

## iv. Tackling Rather Than Avoiding

As Sarah illustrated so clearly, it is very much better to confront things, than to continue to avoid them. If one small step is taken each day, your confidence will improve considerably. But the question is, what to tackle and how much?

## Fig. 4 Formulating a Hierarchy

### Part A: Random listing of difficult activities

Going on an aeroplane
Speaking to a group of people at work
Going on a tram
Trying a new restaurant
Going to the cinema or theatre (particularly if I can't buy the tickets at the end of the row)
Being at football in a big crowd
Sitting through a meeting at work
Going on a train
Waiting in a queue at the bank
Being asked to go on a business trip
Going to a wedding
Going to a party
Being asked away for the weekend to the country
Giving a seminar
Being asked to my girlfriend's place for dinner with her parents

### Part B: The hierarchy

MOST ANXIETY PROVOKING

Going on an aeroplane
Being asked to go on a business trip
Being at football in a big crowd
Going on a train
Being asked away for the weekend to the country
Going to the cinema or theatre (if I can't choose the tickets)
Giving a seminar
Going to a wedding (especially if in the official party)
Trying a new restaurant
Being asked to my girlfriend's place for dinner
Going to a party
Going on a tram
Speaking to a group of people at work
Waiting in a queue at the bank
Sitting through a meeting at work

LEAST ANXIETY PROVOKING

## FORMULATING A HIERARCHY

This can be useful in working out what things need to be dealt with and can be done by listing on a piece of paper any situations or activities which you find difficult to cope with, which are anxiety-provoking, or which you tend to avoid. On another sheet with a vertical line from 'Most Anxiety Provoking' to 'Least Anxiety Provoking', try to order the activities in increasing degrees of difficulty. For example, John (discussed in Chapter 9) randomly drew up a list of activities which he found difficult to tackle. (Refer to Fig. 4, Part A.) He then arranged them in order of difficulty from least to most anxiety-provoking. (Refer to Fig. 4, Part B.) It was important for him to begin dealing with those situations at the bottom which he found to be least difficult (but which still made him anxious); and he gradually moved up the list as he became more confident about those lower down.

In fact, it was necessary for John to formulate several hierarchies from the initial list, breaking the list down into themes, and each task into smaller components. For example, it proved easier for him to go to the cinema if he could choose the tickets than if he could not; and easier for him to tackle sitting through a meeting at work if he didn't say anything, than if he felt he should say something. Breaking each special situation into steps, meant that the number of items on the hierarchy became increasingly large and it was obviously more manageable to have several hierarchies, each one being of increasing order of difficulty. It is also sometimes more encouraging to have several hierarchies of increasing difficulty. This is better than working at the lower end of one for quite a long time. It may also be sensible to have several hierarchies, each with differing themes, which can be worked at in parallel. For example, John was able to tackle, concurrently, three different hierarchies covering the themes: travel, work, and social life.

It depends on you, how you want to arrange, or cluster, the various situations in your hierarchy. The important thing is to change your attitude of avoidance, even if very gradually, and to begin to 'clock up some achievements.'

KEEPING A DIARY

This is an important way of monitoring achievements and seeing whether you are improving – though some people find this arduous. On the other hand, there is no more satisfying way of seeing how you have changed, than to look back a whole year and find that *then* you were pleased to have finally tackled going to the front gate, when yesterday's achievement was returning by train from the country where you had spent a whole week with your sister!

There are several ways of keeping a diary. First, and perhaps most simple, is a 'Dual Diary' system. This is sometimes referred to as the 'Good News and Bad News Diary'. It consists of two sheets of paper or, if using a book, a division of each day into two segments. The first is headed 'Activities and Achievements' (refer to Fig. 5, Part A). On this sheet I ask patients to jot down the date and one particular thing each day they have achieved and feel pleased about. Initially, this may not be anything to do with the specific symptoms, but nonetheless something they feel happy about – for example, knitting two rows in the jumper which has been tucked away incomplete for a year; cleaning up the spare room; finishing a report; or writing a long overdue letter. Any little or large thing will do.

Jot down how you felt, and how well you did the task. Eventually, the activity will become more directly related to the symptoms, as in the example given in Fig. 5. It is sometimes useful, as an incentive, to monitor when you do relaxation exercises and, ideally, a column under R (for Relaxation) should be ticked at least once every day.

The second sheet (the 'Bad News Diary') is headed 'Activities Found Difficult to Tackle or Avoided' (refer to Fig. 5, Part B). In this, it is important to jot down everything you found hard to do, or which you avoided, during the day. It may be that some of your achievements also appear on this part of the diary, because of their anxiety-provoking nature; so, in the right-hand column, try to estimate how much anxiety you experienced during such activities. (If 0 = Calm and Relaxed, and 10 = Sheer Panic, try to list some number on the 0–10 continuum describing how you felt.)

The two sheets, or the two sides of a page, should be kept

together as an ongoing series of notes indicating how you have got on each day. Although some people find this a pedantic and frustrating activity, it is, nevertheless, a most useful way of monitoring whether things have changed; furthermore, it provides an enduring record and means of up-dating the list of things which need to be tackled. It shows how today's difficulties can provide tomorrow's, or next week's, goals!

Frequent repetition in the diary is allowable, as practice is a crucial part of getting better; and any achievement should be repeated, and persisted with, until the activity can be done nonchalantly, without a quiver of anxiety. This can take a considerable amount of time, and a large amount of practice.

If preferred, an alternative to the Dual Diary is the 'Daily Timetable Diary' (refer to Fig. 6). This keeps a record of your activities from the time you wake up in the morning to when you go to sleep at night, and is particularly useful for people who find they are most anxious at certain periods during the day. For example, Mary (introduced in the previous chapter), said she frequently couldn't get herself going in the morning and felt anxious and depressed at that time. On looking at Mary's timetable it became apparent that she had nothing much to look forward to and was not planning her time in any way. She got up at 7.00 a.m. and had a cup of tea on her own; she then sat and had breakfast whilst her husband and the three children got themselves out of the house – they preferred to get their own breakfasts, and she had prepared their lunches the night before. She then mooched around, put the washing on, had another cup of tea, showered and dressed – by which time it was already 9.00 a.m. The morning was fully taken up with making the beds, cleaning up the kitchen, tidying the living and dining rooms, having another cup of tea, and generally feeling bored and depressed. Vacuuming, shopping, ironing and cooking seemed never-ending burdens with no structure to them; they were just ever-present. So, an important aspect of Mary's treatment was the reorganization of her daily timetable, and we decided to use things she enjoyed as incentives and rewards for not-so-pleasureable activities. We experimented with a timetable as follows:

## Fig. 5 The Dual Diary

### PART A: The 'Good News' Diary

| Date | ACTIVITIES AND ACHIEVEMENTS | R | How you felt and how well you did it |
|---|---|---|---|
| 4 . 3 . 86 | Went to the supermarket for the first time in six months | | Felt slightly faint but coped O.K. |
| | | | |
| | | | |

### PART B: The 'Bad News' Diary

| Date | ACTIVITIES YOU FOUND DIFFICULT TO TACKLE OR AVOIDED | ANXIETY (0–10) |
|---|---|---|
| | I could not go into the second shop. | 7 |
| | | |
| | | |

7.00     Get up. Put on the washing. Shower and get dressed.
         Make the bed. (New rule: the children make their own
         beds.)

7.30     Cup of tea. (*Reward*)

7.45     Hang out the washing. Tidy the living and dining rooms.
         Clean up the kitchen after the others leave the house at
         8.15. Do the dishes, etc.

9.00     Breakfast. (*Reward*) Change of diet from toast and jam to
         more sustaining muesli. Read the newspaper. (*Reward*)

9.30-    Vacuum. Try to vacuum most rooms in the half hour. If
10.00    not, postpone remaining rooms until tomorrow.

10.00    Prepare to go out for Yoga lesson.

10.15    Leave home.

10.30    Yoga lesson. (*Reward*)

11.45-   Shopping at the supermarket.
12.30

1.00     Home for lunch (*Reward*) or meet a friend for lunch.
         (*Reward*)


Afternoon mainly free for own activities.


After a time, Mary reported feeling more motivated, energetic and less anxious. Some of you may say, on reading this: 'It's all very well for her. She could actually get to her yoga lesson, go out and do her shopping!' However, this was some time after her treatment began and it had taken Mary a lot of effort to reach the point where she could go to yoga or to the supermarket. Nevertheless, whether or not you are at the stage of venturing out and about, it is crucial to plan your time in order to get the arduous tasks over and done with – rewarding yourself afterwards with something pleasurable (be it a cup of tea, or a TV programme).

A useful supplement to the Daily Timetable Diary is the 'Mastery and Pleasure Diary' (refer to Fig. 7). With this diary you essentially do the same as in the daily timetable; however, beside each activity you put an M and P rating – M standing for Mastery, P for Pleasure. (M rates your competence on a 0–5 scale – 0 referring to no competence at all, and 5 to total competence – while P also rates your enjoyment on a 0–5 scale – 0 for zilch enjoyment and 5 for complete enjoyment.)

*Fig. 6* **The Daily Timetable Diary**

| HOUR/DAY | MONDAY | TUESDAY | WEDNESDAY | THURSDAY | FRIDAY | SATURDAY | SUNDAY |
|---|---|---|---|---|---|---|---|
| 7.00 | | | | | | | |
| 8.00 | | | | | | | |
| 9.00 | | | | | | | |
| 10.00 | | | | | | | |
| 11.00 | | | | | | | |
| 12.00 | | | | | | | |
| 1.00 | | | | | | | |
| 2.00 | | | | | | | |
| 3.00 | | | | | | | |
| 4.00 | | | | | | | |
| 5.00 | | | | | | | |
| 6.00 | | | | | | | |
| 7.00 | | | | | | | |
| 8.00 | | | | | | | |
| 9.00 | | | | | | | |
| 10.00 | | | | | | | |
| 11.00 | | | | | | | |
| TOTAL | | | | | | | |

*Fig. 7* **Mastery and Pleasure Diary**

| HOUR/DAY | MONDAY | | TUESDAY | | WEDNESDAY | | THURSDAY | | FRIDAY | | SATURDAY | | SUNDAY | |
|---|---|---|---|---|---|---|---|---|---|---|---|---|---|---|
| | M | P | M | P | M | P | M | P | M | P | M | P | M | P |
| 7.00 | | | | | | | | | | | | | | |
| 8.00 | | | | | | | | | | | | | | |
| 9.00 | | | | | | | | | | | | | | |
| 10.00 | | | | | | | | | | | | | | |
| 11.00 | | | | | | | | | | | | | | |
| 12.00 | | | | | | | | | | | | | | |
| 1.00 | | | | | | | | | | | | | | |
| 2.00 | | | | | | | | | | | | | | |
| 3.00 | | | | | | | | | | | | | | |
| 4.00 | | | | | | | | | | | | | | |
| 5.00 | | | | | | | | | | | | | | |
| 6.00 | | | | | | | | | | | | | | |
| 7.00 | | | | | | | | | | | | | | |
| 8.00 | | | | | | | | | | | | | | |
| 9.00 | | | | | | | | | | | | | | |
| 10.00 | | | | | | | | | | | | | | |
| 11.00 | | | | | | | | | | | | | | |
| TOTAL | | | | | | | | | | | | | | |

Rating scales    M = 'mastery' (i.e. competence at the activity attempted)   0 (nil) – 5 (complete)
                 P = 'pleasure' (i.e. enjoyment of the activity attempted)   0 (nil) – 5 (complete)

The M&P Diary is useful for some people, because it highlights the fact that, though they might have felt sluggish during the day, they did do at least one thing well. On the other hand, it may prove to be a useful reminder of an all-too-well-known fact – that they are doing little that is enjoyable, and that it is time to start reading again for a quarter of an hour a day, or writing letters, or telephoning a friend, or learning to play tennis, etc (i.e. incorporating more enjoyable activities into their lives).

The form of any of the diaries used may be determined both by its purpose and by what you feel to be most comfortable. It is important, however, that you motivate yourself to keep one sort or another, for even a small (2in square) pocket diary will do as a means of jotting down one thing a day that has been tackled.

# Chapter 11

# Resolving Underlying Issues

As was discussed in Chapter 8, an important part of getting better entails working through the underlying issues that led to the cumulative tension in the first place. But how, first of all, do you become aware of what some of the issues might be?

Some patients have a clear recollection of the time when their problems began and what seemed, on the surface at least, to cause them. For example, one of my patients called Penny knew that her first panic came soon after the death of her mother. She was thirty-nine and her mother had died of cancer after a painful illness lasting two years; the responsibility of looking after her had been mostly Penny's and she had found this very stressful. However, in talking about her life, it became apparent that Penny had had problems earlier than this. She had been a middle child between an adored and successful older brother and a bright and pretty younger sister. She had felt inadequate and excluded, and had never learnt to stand up for herself – largely through fear of being disliked. This was one of the reasons she had been left with the care of her dying mother, as she had been unable to insist that her brother and sister provide an equal amount of help.

On the other hand, some patients seem totally unaware of what their anxiety is related to. Fear of the symptoms themselves, and the perpetual worry about whether a panic attack will occur, act as a mask for more deep-seated insecurities. For many of these people, the symptoms provide a defence. It may be too frightening, for instance, or too guilt- inducing, to contemplate that your marriage is not ideal; or that you have, as long as you can remember, been angry with your parents. In such cases, the anxiety attacks act both as a symptom of, and defence against, underlying issues.

This is not to suggest that for all agoraphobics the symptoms are a defence. In some, they may be merely a residue of stress, fatigue or illness; however, in all cases, it is useful to understand the actual historical context in which the symptoms have arisen. In my treatment of patients I use three main questionnaires to enable both them and me to gain a picture of their background; and it may be useful for you to fill out two of these, in order to place your own problems in context. They are:

1. A Life History Questionnaire
2. A Problem Definition Sheet, and
3. A Life Line, or Autobiography Sheet.

The Life History Questionnaire requires a comprehensive account of: general information (age, date of birth, height, weight, etc); details of referral and previous treatment; fears and negative thoughts; marital status and nature of present household; family history; educational history; interests; employment history; sexual and health history; and any other aspects of present behaviour that are worth commenting on. This may be too complex to be of any great use in the present context, and much of this information will emerge, anyway, through the other two questionnaires set out below.

The purpose of the Problem Definition and Life Line sheets is to gain a clearer picture of how your life has evolved to the present, and where you wish to be going in the future. It helps some patients to visualize this in the form of a diagram (refer to Fig. 8), and I outline the task to patients as follows:

i.  If you think about your life, you think in terms of the PAST (point *a.* on the diagram), the PRESENT (point *b.*), and the FUTURE (point *c.*). There are different options in the future and different paths to choose from – *c.* refers to a number of alternative branching paths indicating these different possibilities.

The way in which you describe the symptoms of panic and anxiety suggests that the present is tangled, and this makes you feel trapped. This is represented by the tangle in *b.* You are right in the middle of this tangle (represented by the dot in the middle of *b.*).

Now, in answering these questionnaires, I want you to step out of the present (to point *d.*), and to take an overview of the past, the present and the possibilities in the future. The answers to the questions will be painting and framing a picture of your life as you see it.

Fig. 8 therefore provides a visual representation of what you will be trying to portray in your answers to the questions.

## Fig. 8 'My Life As I See It'

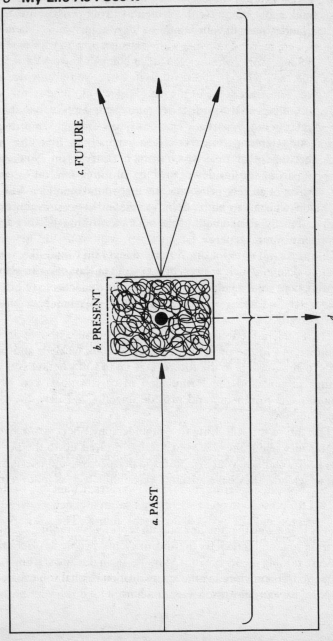

ii. To fill in the Problem Definition Sheet (refer to Fig. 9) try to think about the present. Elements of your present life are: your relationship with your family – with your husband and children if you are married or living with someone, or with your parents and siblings; work (whether you are at home or at work); friendships; interests; feelings about yourself; where you are living; money, etc. These are some of the many aspects of the present. Now try to outline what you feel are your central problems at present (refer to Fig. 9, part *a*.). Obviously, this will include an outline of your symptoms, but try to look generally at your life to see if there are other areas which worry or distress you. Now, move on to part *b*. and jot down anything you find difficult to tackle or which is anxiety-provoking, or that you avoid. This will enable you to formulate a hierarchy, as outlined in the previous chapter.

Finally, think about goals, both short term (specific) and long term (more general: i.e. how you want your life to turn out) (part *c*.). Try to jot down those things you would like to be able to do and which at present you feel you can't. Write also about options you would like to pursue in the future. (This clearly refers, as well, to point *c*. in Fig. 8 – as has been discussed already.)

The Problem Definition Sheet is useful because it gives an outline of difficulties in the present, what needs to be tackled, and possible goals to aim towards in the future. It is up to you whether you wish to change or not; and the formulation of certain goals can help you choose paths to pursue, and provide impetus and new directions in which to move.

The aim of the Life Line or Autobiography Sheet[1] is to give you a clearer idea about the way your life has evolved up to the present. It also helps you place your symptoms in perspective, and possibly allows you to see how they have arisen. I explain the task as follows (refer to Fig. 10 ).

Try to imagine that the line or path represents your life . . . Starting from your childhood, try to think of events, people or places that were turning points for you. Mark these on the line starting from the top, and mentioning the age or year at which they occurred . . . Now, for example, when were you born? (Jot down your birth date

118

*Fig. 9* **Problem Definition Sheet**

a. Write a brief description of what you feel your central problems are at present:

b. List any activities or situations which you find difficult to tackle, anxiety provoking, or that you avoid:

c. List if possible the aims or goals towards which you wish to work (e.g. what you would like to be able to do which at present you can't, and how you want your life to be in the future):

---

in the top left-hand corner.) So, your story starts off with 'I was born . . .' Were there any family myths or stories about your birth? (For instance, did your parents want a boy or girl? Was the birth painful? Were you early or late?) Jot this down too . . . Now, what is your first memory? Try to remember the earliest thing, even if you are not sure whether it is a 'real' memory, or derived from photos.

119

Jot this down, and the age and year at which it occurrred . . . Now, continue to write down any events that you remember. It doesn't matter how small or large they are. Try to put down as much as you can. Essentially, you will be writing your autobiography . . . Now, in parallel with the events on the left-hand side, try to write down, on the right-hand side, whether there were any problems which arose at the times mentioned. (For example, some people feel shy when they first go to school. Others get depressed in adolescence, etc.) One important thing to jot down will be the emergence of your first panic attack, and what events were going on in your life at that time – or had just preceded it. Continue your account until the present, and then try to outline what help you feel you need. If you have referred yourself to a therapist or counsellor, outline the events leading up to this.

Some people find filling in the Life Line/Autobiography Sheet a very hard thing to do. They may delay writing until they feel ready to face aspects about their past which seem frightening or depressing; and it can even be true that their symptoms keep thoughts about the past at bay. On the whole, however, most people find it an enlightening and revealing exercise. The accounts given by Jenny, Liz, and Peter in Chapter 2 provide examples of how people's symptoms become more explicable once they are looked at in the context of the individual histories. In fact, the Life Line enabled them not only to get an overview of their lives, but started the process of releasing emotions that had been bottled up for years. Some people cry whilst writing their life history and feel great relief afterwards. It can help to read it out and discuss it with someone. If there is no one with whom you feel you can do this, then find a counsellor or therapist who can help you work through it.

The main aim of doing the Problem Definition Sheet and Life Line/Autobiography Sheet is to gain a clear picture (as in Fig. 8) of the past, the present and the future. New perspectives and directions will emerge from the task, and it may highlight issues that need to be worked on. For example, you may realize that shyness or lack of assertiveness have been perpetual themes in your life. You may find there are difficulties in your marriage that need to be addressed. Or you may decide that it is time to aim towards going back to work or

## Fig. 10  Your Life Line/Autobiography

Imagine the line below represents your life. Starting from your childhood, can you think of events, people or places that were turning points for you? Mark these on the line starting from the top, mentioning the age or year at which these occurred. Also mark in things that were important to you at different times and show how these led to where you are now. Try to describe each thing in as much detail as possible. (Use more sheets and continue the line yourself if you run out of space.)

*For example*:

AGE     YEAR
            20/1/45 . . . I was born

2½        1947 . . . I remember being on the verandah of my
                       parents first house in a pushchair

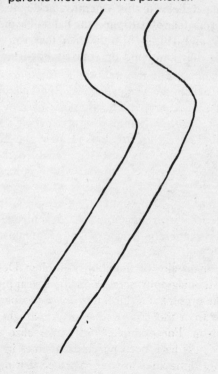

further study, and that you have been at home with three children for long enough. Numerous themes can arise, and these need to be faced directly. If you feel you need help with your problems, be they individual or marital problems, then get help. Find out whether there are good counsellors or therapists in the area, and refer yourself to one of them.

If you find after a couple of sessions that rapport is lacking, then look for another counsellor; you need to find someone with whom you feel at ease, and with whom you can talk. But make sure they are qualified and fully registered. Looking for a therapist is rather like 'shopping' for the most useful techniques – as mentioned in Chapters 9 and 10. Certain counsellors suit some people, others work for others; and you must find one who suits YOU. Keep in mind, however, that working through underlying difficulties is only one aspect of the problem. In parallel with this, you must tackle the symptoms directly to counteract your fear of panic and the habit of avoidance (as outlined in Chapters 9 and 10). It is only then that you will overcome your agoraphobia fully and build up your confidence and self-esteem.

*Chapter 12*

# Building Your Confidence
# And Self-Esteem

As discussed in Chapter 9, the development of confidence and self-esteem occurs as a by-product of, and in parallel with, understanding, learning to relax, counteracting negative thoughts, and dealing with things you have been avoiding. However, there are various ways of enhancing your confidence as time goes by. As you begin to tackle things and jot them down in your Achievements Diary, you will begin to perceive that, not only are things changing as you are able to do more, but that you are beginning to feel different as well. It is important to monitor these changes, adding your perception of what has changed weekly or fortnightly to a list of 'Things that have changed'. (Refer to Fig. 11).

For example, Sarah (discussed in Chapter 10) was able to say at the end of her first week of treatment:

> I've been to the front gate every day since seeing you, and yesterday
> I was able to stand on the verandah and watch the world go by
> before going in . . . I've been back to the supermarket and walked
> slowly through the area where I had my first panic. I was able to
> slow down, and I didn't hurry back to the car. I got in slowly after a
> pause, and didn't have to use my puffer.

In her second session, she formulated a list of things that had changed during the previous week (refer to Fig. 11, part *a*.) Her improvement was, indeed, remarkable. All I can say is that she is a very 'gutsy' and courageous 71-year-old woman, who wants to enjoy the rest of her life (and that includes defeating the panic).

Many people find that it takes much longer than a week to build up a list this long. However, each time something changes, it is important to add it to the list. These changes can include, for example, 'I've finally finished the jumper I've been knitting for three years'; 'I've taught

## *Fig. 11* **List of Things That Have Changed**

*a.* Sarah (after her first week of treatment):

1. I've learnt to relax.
2. I've been to the gate every day and enjoyed it.
3. I've stopped on the verandah and watched the world go by.
4. I've been back to the supermarket.
5. I'm learning to slow down and be calmer.
6. I feel more confident than I did a week ago.
7. I'm beginning to understand things better.
8. I'm not as afraid of the panic as I used to be.

*b.* Jenny (part of her list after a year of treatment):

1. I'm now able to go into small shops and supermarkets and not worry about standing in the queue.
2. I don't shake when I hand over change any more.
3. I've learnt to relax completely, even at work.
4. I've been more assertive with my boss, and stated calmly that I want to work only four days a week. (He has accepted this, and we've arranged for a replacement from within the company.)
5. I'm now able to travel a few stops by tube, and plan to increase this.
6. I've joined a health club and have started exercising again.
7. I now go out to lunch with my work friends again.
8. I play golf with my husband on my day off and don't feel nervous out on the course.
9. I feel very much more confident generally.
10. We've been to the theatre and ballet on a couple of occasions and I've enjoyed going out again.
11. I now know that I have the power to change things, and no one except me can do it.
12. My attitude is more positive.
13. I have many more plans for the future.

myself a new piece on the piano'; 'I have driven round the block for the first time in six months'; 'I feel more optimistic about things'; 'My attitude seems to be more positive than a month ago'; 'I'm beginning to plan more'.

Jenny (discussed in Chapter 3), had a long list after a year of treatment. (She came once weekly for the first four months, and then at less regular intervals, tapering off to once every six weeks until treatment finally concluded.) Part of her list is included in Fig. 11, part *b*. and highlights the numerous areas she had been working on. The most important thing is that you keep a running tally of any little shifts in your behaviour, attitudes, or feelings. You will soon find that they begin to add up.

In parallel with this list, it is important to keep an evolving set of 'Goals': both short term and long term. These may be both specific and general. Returning to Sarah and Jenny again, their goals (paralleling their previous lists of things that have changed), are set out in Fig. 12. They are working on different things. Sarah is at an earlier stage than Jenny – though some people may feel well behind Sarah's level. However, no matter where you are with regard to goals, it is important to break them down into *small* steps and tackle things one at a time. If you want to drive your car again, practise sitting in it first, and learn to cope with the anxiety at that level before going on. If you want to walk around the block, go to the gate first, and then to the post box and *practise*, before moving on to the next stage. To stand at the front door for five minutes can be just as important an achievement as to get on a plane for the first time. *Value* your achievements and practise them repeatedly. You will soon find that your attitude begins to change.

You will probably find that you encounter *setbacks* during the process of getting better. It is important to remember that these are a normal part of the process and not something to be despaired at. Try not to let your confidence be 'knocked for six' by them. Some people find that improvement is rather slow at first, as they start learning to relax, counteracting the thoughts and tackling activities. They then begin to experience times when they feel better in themselves, and they are greatly encouraged by this. Eventually they find they have a day when they feel better than they have for ages, and so they can attempt more activities. However, the following day they may find that they feel worse than they have in a long while. Mary (referred to in Chapters 9 and 10) gives an example of this:

## *Fig. 12* **Goals**

*a.* Sarah:

1. I would like to be able to walk to the corner shop on my own.
2. I would like to feel more relaxed when friends come to visit me.
3. I would like to be able to visit friends without having to worry where the loo is (I fear wetting myself).
4. I would like to go on a day's drive with my husband.
5. I would dearly love to visit my sister in the country. (I would have to go by train.)

*b.* Jenny

1. I would like to make clear decisions on what I want to do and then *do it*.
2. I want to make every post a winning post.
3. I want to work on getting my confidence back even more.
4. I want to learn how to keep a positive attitude at all times and not just sometimes.
5. I want to practise my interaction with people close to me, so that they take more notice of me and respect my point of view.
6. I want to spend half an hour reading the paper every day and be more informed. (I will start with 5 minutes!)
7. I want to enrol part-time in further study next year and work towards a degree.
8. I want to feel completely confident in the tube, so I will have to practise it.
9. I would eventually like to fly on an aeroplane again.

---

On Monday, I felt better than I had for months. I even walked to the hairdresser's and felt quite calm whilst I sat having my hair done. Previously I would have been frightened of panicking and of wanting to scream out of the shop with my hair half done. Anyway, afterwards, I rang a friend, and we met for lunch near the hairdresser's, and it was super. I felt confident and didn't shake at all. But do you know, the next day, I could hardly drag myself out of

## *Fig. 13* **The Path of Improvement**

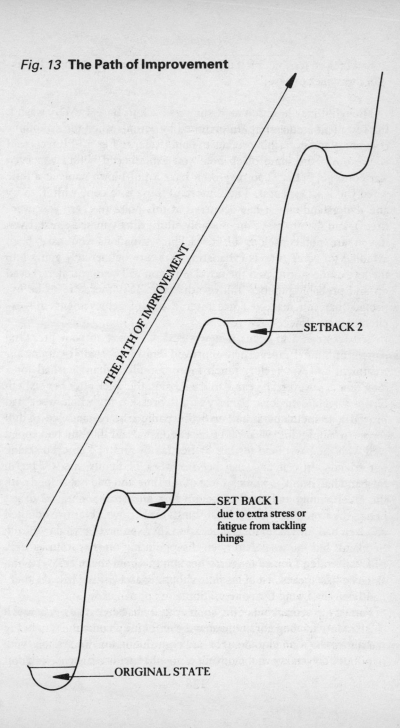

THE PATH OF IMPROVEMENT

SETBACK 2

SET BACK 1
due to extra stress or
fatigue from tackling
things

ORIGINAL STATE

bed I felt so terrible. I felt dizzy and shaky all morning, and it felt as if I was back to base 1!

Though it may have felt as if she was back to Base 1, Mary wasn't. Improvement is sometimes interrupted by periods when the symptoms re-emerge and everything seems to halt. (Refer to Fig. 13.) It feels as if you're down the same black hole you experienced before you even started to get better. You may even have a full-blown panic at a time when you least expect it. The important thing is to cope with it, to try and understand why it has occurred at this point (e.g. are you over-tired?), and then to move on, possibly after giving yourself a rest. Even if you are not conscious of it, tackling situations you have been avoiding for some time is exhausting. You are deliberately going into the 'eye of the storm', and the novel situation will keep you alert, keyed up and probably pumped full of adrenalin. It is therefore to be expected that you may well tire after a day of achievement and excitement; so, if necessary, rest.

Setbacks can also occur if new stresses emerge in your life. One patient of mine, Frances, had improved considerably after coming for treatment and was feeling much more confident than she had for a long time. However, she came into a session the week after her sixtieth birthday feeling anxious, panicky and depressed; the whole week had proved a tremendous strain, and the panic had re-emerged in full force. In 'unpacking' what had happened, she said that she had coped well with the party held for her by her family and had enjoyed seeing her friends. But, it had also been a week of family crises. Her ill husband had drunk too much most of the time and had not helped with the entertaining, and she had begun to realize that if she was to get better she would have to do most things on her own. Her two adopted children had turned up for the occasion (her son had flown down from Scotland) but the week had been disappointing on that front as well. She had looked forward to seeing her son to whom she felt closest; but, since he had spent most of his time shopping and visiting friends, there had been little time for conversation.

Part of her setback was due, as she put it, to 'bereavement'. She felt she had lost any hope of her husband ever being a companion to her in the things she wanted to do. (He had come along for two sessions with her, but had shown no motivation to change or to help with her problems.) She also felt she had to face the fact that she was not as close to her children as she would have liked to be. Another thing had also become apparent: that she was under-assertive and needed to be more open and honest with her feelings. The thought, for example, that she could have asked her son to come out with her for lunch one day had not crossed her mind. After honestly facing these various issues over the next couple of weeks, Frances began to improve again. She organized outings with her friends (of whom she had several close ones), and enrolled for a course on local history. For her, the setback was a response to a stressful turning point in her life.

It is important to respond constructively to setbacks, whether they are caused by fatigue or by additional stresses which can occur during times that you are improving. Try to see them as a test, but not an undermining, of your confidence.

For many patients, particularly those who are housebound, their tension, anxiety and panic are largely by-products of the frustration, boredom and loneliness created by their lifestyle. Young mothers who feel trapped by the never-ending round of nappy-washing and attending to the demands of a two-year-old, can find that frustration becomes overlaid with fear if their tension approaches the point of panic. This is a hellish 'Catch 22' situation; they can't get out because of fear of panic, and the more they are stuck at home the more likely they are to panic. It is crucial that this vicious circle be broken in some way. One way is to develop one new interest; this may be undertaken at home or away from home (crochet or swimming lessons, for example), but it is most important that it be something new. Mary (discussed in Chapters 9 and 10) started yoga. Mike (discussed in Chapter 1) learnt meditation. Both of them found the new activity useful, not only because it was something new and interesting, but because it also supplemented the relaxation procedures outlined in Chapter 10.

An excellent way of deciding upon at least one new interest is to have a 'brainstorming' session and fill in the 'Interest and Hobbies List' with as many ideas as you can think of. (Refer to Fig 14.) It doesn't matter whether they are interests you used to have but have dropped, ideas gleaned from magazines that you have always wanted to try, or totally fantastic ambitions that you have dreamed of for years. Jot them all down. Then choose one, and only one, to begin with. But make it manageable.

Some patients say to me 'But what will I choose?' and 'How do I know that I will enjoy it?' The simple answer to the second question is: 'You don't!'; and to the first: 'Choose whatever appeals to you most', but remember that developing a new interest is often a matter of trial and

---

*Fig. 14* **Interests and Hobbies List**


*List any interests or hobbies etc. that you would like to develop:*

*a.* AT HOME: (for example)

1. reading
2. sewing
3. knitting
4. carpentry
5. painting . . .
6.
7.
8.
9.
10.
11.
12.

*b.* AWAY FROM HOME: (for example)

1. cycling
2. tennis
3. theatre
4. cinema
5. evening classes . . .
6.
7.
8.
9.
10.
11.
12.

---

error. Some people find it worthwhile, as their first choice of a new activity, to join a self-help group in the community; as meeting others with similar problems can provide added confidence to go on and tackle other things. (A list of some of these self-help groups is given in Appendix C at the back of the book.)

Developing new activities and interests helps many people to find a heightened sense of self-confidence. If boredom and frustration seem to be important background factors, then taking this course of action is crucial. On the other hand, there are certain individuals whose perpetual hyper-activity is one of the sources of stress. (This issue was touched upon briefly in Chapter 9 when the phenomenon of 'relaxation-induced-anxiety' was discussed.) For such people, cutting down on activities and developing alternative or fewer interests is crucial. Learning just to 'be', rather than to 'do', is essential, and relaxation and meditation can help in this.

For some other people, developing self-confidence and self-esteem may be helped by, or result in, readjustment of priorities given to different areas of their lives. Indeed, part of getting better may require an overhaul of lifestyle. John, for example (discussed in Chapter 9), found that the manic energy with which he tackled new projects in his computer company left him exhausted and drained in all other areas of his life. He seemed to have two paces at work: 'flat out' and 'stop'. When he stopped, tension and fatigue would catch up with him; the panics would get worse, his relationship with his girlfriend would suffer, he didn't want to see his other friends. And, when he was flat out, he didn't have time for these other things anyway!

One useful way for you to make an analysis of your lifestyle, as it is at present, is to look at the different aspects of your life and evaluate whether they are as you would like them to be. By doing this, you can begin to formulate goals and objectives towards which you would like to aim. Fig. 15 sets out several major areas, moving from the more general to more particular aspects. It may help if you draw this up on a larger sheet of paper and fill it out.

It is important to note not only what you want to change in specific areas, but also what balance you would like to achieve between the different areas themselves. Gaining an overview enables you to set objectives and make freeing changes in the balance of your activities.

131

## Fig. 15 Formulation of Goals and Objectives

GENERAL AREAS FOR CHANGE

| | Things I like about myself | Things I dislike about myself and would like to change | Goals and objectives |
|---|---|---|---|
| Myself | | | |
| My situation | Things I like about my present situation | Things I dislike about my present situation and would like to change | Goals and objectives |

## SPECIFIC AREAS FOR CHANGE

| | Aspects I like | Aspects I dislike and would like to change | Goals and objectives |
|---|---|---|---|
| 1. *Relationships:* a) intimate (if at present involved) | | | Goals and objectives |
| b) with family | Things I am comfortable with | Things I am uncomfortable with and would like to change | Goals and objectives |
| c) with friends (social life) | Friends I like<br><br>Things I like doing with them | Problems (difficulties in social situations, etc.) | Goals and objectives |

| | Things I like | Things I dislike and would like to change | Goals and objectives |
|---|---|---|---|
| 2. Work | | | |
| 3. Leisure | Interests and activities that I enjoy (now and in the past) | Any difficulties with leisure | Goals and objectives |
| | | | |

| 4. Other practical areas | Positives | Problems (aspects to change) | Goals and objectives |
|---|---|---|---|
| a) accommodation | | | |
| b) financial | | | |
| c) appearance (personal, wardrobe, etc.) | | | |

| 5. Any other problem areas (e.g. bad habits or compulsions you want to work on) | Problems | Goals and objectives |
|---|---|---|
| | | |

# RESOLUTIONS

| Areas for change | Specific goals/tasks | When? Date |
|---|---|---|
| 1. Relationships<br> Intimate | | |
| Family | | |
| Friends | | |
| 2. Work | | |
| 3. Leisure | | |
| 4. Other practical areas:<br><br> a) accommodation<br><br> b) financial<br><br> c) appearance | | |
| 5. Other problem areas | | |

In fact, some people find that setting goals and monitoring achievements in this way can help in building up confidence. On the other hand, it may be that this 'tight schedule' becomes arduous and constraining – in which case, if it doesn't help, cease doing it. As with all other areas mentioned in previous chapters, you must choose what works best for you in building up confidence and self-esteem.

## Chapter 13

# Three Treatment Case Studies

The previous five chapters (Chapter 8–12) provide a framework for treatment, indicating the different components necessary for recovery. Each scheme always seems more useful when you can see directly how it works. I will, therefore, take you through Jenny's treatment in more detail in this chapter, to illustrate how the framework is used. Liz and Peter's treatment will also be discussed generally at the end of the chapter.

## Jenny's Treatment

SESSION I.

The treatment of Jenny, whose life history is outlined in Chapter 2, began with her describing her symptoms, how they had begun, and the reason why she wanted treatment. I then explained to her in general terms how agoraphobia as a condition develops (as detailed in Fig. 2 in Chapter 8). The rationale behind treatment was then outlined to her as follows:

> The aim of treatment is to enable you to learn to cope with the feelings of panic you have been experiencing. Through learning and practising relaxation techniques, and through changing your fearful thoughts about the panic, you will gradually be able to tackle the situations you have been avoiding. You may find initially that panic comes over you in these situations. Your immediate impulse will be to flee, and to avoid what you fear will be the consequences of the panic. (Jenny feared collapsing in public. Others fear fainting, having a heart attack, wetting themselves or defecating in public, or going mad.) However, it is only by learning to stay with the panic: calming yourself down and remaining in the

138

situation until the feelings begin to pass, that you will prove to yourself that nothing disastrous will happen. It is not the situation that causes the feelings, but your own perception of being trapped and helpless in that situation. This perception causes anxiety. You then begin to fear this anxiety will harm you, or result in you losing control. This second fear causes the anxiety to mount, and lo-and-behold, you have caused your own panic attack. It is therefore your own perceptions and feelings that need to be dealt with. The situation itself (be it in a tram, train, shop or on an escalator) is not the problem.

Eventually, through tackling the situations where you experience panic (some or many of which you may have been avoiding), you will gradually find yourself able to cope with the feelings. By slowing down, relaxing, taking deep breaths and learning to think: 'the feelings will not harm me, they are not dangerous; nothing worse will happen . . .', you will find that the anxiety will begin to subside. Eventually, through practice, you will learn to be panic-free in many or all situations. It takes hard work, practice and determination to overcome the problem. However, paradoxically, the hard work needs to be done in ways other than those we have been taught. You cannot do it by gritting your teeth and stoically going after success. You need rather to work hard at unwinding, relaxing, learning to slow down rather than speed up. You need to learn to 'be' with yourself, rather than 'do-ing' and frenetically pursuing activity all the time.

Towards the end of the first session, Jenny was given the three assessment questionnaires outlined in Chapter 11 (the Problem Definition Sheet, the Life History Questionnaire and the Life Line or Autobiography Sheet). These were to be done for homework. I also recommended that she read Claire Weekes' book on agoraphobia and Wayne Dyer's book (see page 95). Finally, the session ended with my giving her a summary sheet on 'The Steps in the Treatment of Agoraphobia' (refer to Fig. 16), which is designed to give you a clearer idea of how to start your treatment, and to monitor its progress.

## *Fig. 16* **Steps in the Treatment of Agoraphobia**

PHASE I (parallelling phase II)

*1st Step: Understanding* (refer to Fig. 2)

    a) the background factors
    b) symptoms

*2nd Step: Acceptance of the condition*

PHASE II: PRACTICAL STRATEGIES

1. Relaxation
2. Techniques to counteract panic attacks:
    a) 'Ten Golden Rules'
    b) Relaxation-strategies
    c) Coping statements chosen by yourself

3. Non-avoidance as a general approach or principle:
    a) Formulate a hierarchy of anxiety-evoking situations.
    b) Break each situation down into small steps.
    c) Begin to tackle them at your own pace. (The pace varies for each individual. Flooding may be chosen by some.)
    d) Try to do things even when you feel you can't or don't want to.

4. Keep a diary, listing achievements each day, and things avoided.
5. Retrospectively evaluate things that have changed so that you can see how you have improved.
6. Formulate goals: both short term (things to tackle) and long term.
7. Learn to differentiate between what you really want to do and what you feel has been imposed upon you.
8. Practise assertion.
9. Generate your own list of coping/encouraging statements for:
    a) Coping with panic
    b) General assertion

10. Develop interests.
11. Try to establish a way in which you feel needed and wanted (e.g. by being concerned for others: the group may help in this respect).

*Add any further points that you think may help*

e.g.: Exercise reduces tendency to panic.
      Smoking and coffee contribute to tendency to panic.

SESSION 2.

One week later, Jenny had completed the long questionnaires and had read most of Claire Weekes' book. Her account of her life history gave considerable insight into the causes of her initial tension, and the panic which had occurred three-and-a-half years previously. (This account is contained in her response to the Problem Definition Sheet and Life Line which are presented in Chapter 3.) She began to talk about her early life, reading her life history out to me. It became apparent that, even when she was very young, she had been anxious and dependent, and was encouraged by her parents to be 'seen and not heard' and to be 'a good little girl'. The death of her grandmother who had lived with them and who had loved Jenny unconditionally, left her isolated. Further, she was an only child who lacked the company of other children of her own age.

Jenny began to see that perhaps her anxieties had been deep-seated, only emerging fully when she experienced her first panic attack. She also perceived that from an early age she had been discouraged from being assertive and stating her own opinions. She was frightened of her parents' disapproval, and did as much as she could to please them.

We did not finish discussing her life history in this session, as it was important to move on to practical strategies that she could practise and use during the following week. We therefore went through the Progressive Relaxation Techniques outlined in Chapter 10. She was given a written copy of the exercises and was asked to make her own audio-cassette tape by reading the exercises into a recorder (at this stage, I did not have any ready-made tapes available). She was also asked to keep the Dual Diary, also described in Chapter 10, in order to monitor a single achievement each day, to tick the days on which she practised relaxation, and to jot down those things which she found anxiety-provoking. Finally, she was given a list of the 'Ten Golden Rules' (also outlined in Chapter 10); I encouraged her to read them frequently and to carry them round with her in her handbag.

SESSION 3.

She came to the third session having practised her relaxation exercises every day. She said that she was looking forward to progress but was still feeling shaky.

The main triumph during the week was that she had spoken to her mother on the phone in a way she had never done before. Her mother had rung up on the Friday night complaining that Jenny had not been to visit them for more than a week and Jenny had been able to respond assertively that she was busy during the weekend but would try to call in one night during the following week on her way home from work. Her mother had been put out by this, though she had accepted it.

On the other hand, Jenny had been confused and depressed about her work situation. Although her boss had retired, he had continued to work in an honorary capacity in the same company and also on the board and council of several government and non-government organizations. Thus, the pace of work as his secretary had not abated and she felt that she would not be able to cope if she did not have more time off. She had also wanted to discuss with him again the possibility of her working four days a week (which involved finding a typist from within the company to help him on Wednesdays), but she did not know how she could do this.

Her symptoms had not improved much. She was still shaky on her car trips to and from work; and even in the office she felt panicky, though the relaxation exercises had helped to some extent. We spent most of the session talking through these issues from the previous week, and for some of the remaining time we returned to the life history and discussed her adult years. It became even more apparent that lack of assertiveness was one of the major factors contributing to her overall tension. Both with her parents and her boss there had been a history of pleasing them at the expense of her own wishes and needs; and her marriage had been delayed for many years, partly because of fear of her parents' disapproval. In addition, her lack of higher education was a direct result of her father's perception that this was not appropriate for women. Her perpetual exhaustion during the past thirteen years had been due to the unmitigating demands of her boss, her inability to set limits, and her wish to please both him and her family.

SESSION 4.

The following week she came in feeling shaky and low. She had not gone to work that morning as she had felt too unwell. The pace of work had not decreased and she had been unable to ask for time off. She had practised the relaxation every day and at the weekend had tried to go into the local shop to buy some milk. She had felt very faint at the counter and had scurried out once she had been served. However, she was pleased that she had attempted to go to the shop and had felt slightly more confident as a result.

Once again, the main issue seemed to be lack of assertiveness and we discussed ways in which she could ask for three weeks off – this being a long-overdue holiday. We role-played her request several times before the end of the session and I also suggested that she read *When I Say No I Feel Guilty* (see page 95), as a way of gaining ideas about assertiveness.

SESSION 5.

Jenny was one week into her three-week holiday by the time I saw her next. Her boss had phoned to ask her how she was on the day of our previous session and she had taken courage and said 'I'd like to take some leave'. She had felt relieved at having done this, and he had responded positively. He had rung again five days later to see how she was getting on and she had said 'When I return, I would like us to discuss the possibility of our arranging a temporary assistant from within the company to take my place on Wednesdays'. He had agreed to consider this. During the week off she had slept, practised the relaxation, read a lot, and begun to feel more confident about the trip to the local shop. She had practised the trip on several occasions and had not shaken as much as before whilst at the counter. She had consciously used the relaxation procedure both walking there and while standing inside.

She talked at length about her background saying that she had consistently felt inferior to other people. Her parents had always disapproved of things she had done on her own initiative; and they hadn't allowed her to do what other girlfriends at school had been allowed to do. When she was little she wasn't allowed to go and play with others in the street. Her lack of confidence developed at this time and she said: 'It seems that I've always needed someone to reassure me.' Even when she was offered her job as secretary to the managing director, she did not readily accept the position and had to be persuaded to do so. She felt angry about her timidity and the way in which her parents had brought her up.

At the end of the session, after some discussion, I suggested that one way of getting in touch with the feelings of anger she had expressed so clearly was to sit down and write a letter to her parents indicating how she felt about them. The letter was to be as angry as she felt, allowing her to explore all the feelings she had repressed. It was not to be a letter to put in the post, but one in which she could articulate the forbidden and hidden parts of herself as honestly as possible. We would discuss it during the next session. She said she would find it extremely difficult to be so honest about her parents in such a negative way, and she even felt guilty at the thought of it. I said that having 'shoulds' about feelings ('I "should" not be angry with the ones I love') was like having a lid on the pressure cooker. If there is no open acknowledgement of our negative feelings, they build up inside until the pressure is great enough for them to burst out in fits of aggression – or, as in Jenny's case, in panic attacks. Many people find that unacknowledged and/or unexpressed feelings give rise to depression. Indeed, we bind up much of our energy in repressing the negative feelings we don't want to acknowledge, or feel we 'should' not have; and this then prevents us from achieving our full potential.

SESSION 6.

Jenny had attempted quite a few things by the next time I saw her. She had been to the hairdresser's and had had her hair waved. This was a tremendous achievement, as it required sitting for several hours whilst her hair was cut and permed; she had previously feared having a panic in the middle of a hair cut and running out of the shop with only one side done! (This is a frequent fear in agoraphobics.) She had used the relaxation procedures to calm herself down; she had the 'Ten Golden Rules' in her handbag; and she had occupied herself by reading *Vogue* during the times when she was not engaged in conversation. She had felt exhilarated afterwards and had gone to the supermarket with her husband on the strength of it the following day when, again, she found herself able to cope.

She could not understand why, if she could still get herself to-and-from work, she found many other tasks so difficult. We then discussed the fact that her car provided her with an extension of her own home, rather like the shell on the back of a snail. Because of this she felt relatively comfortable in it; she certainly still shook and felt panicky when caught at traffic lights, but on the whole she felt safe and in control. However, because in other situations she felt trapped and unable to get away quickly, she therefore feared the possibility of panic more.

We also discussed a game of golf which she had played with her husband during the week. Initially she had felt very uneasy, despite his presence which usually reassured her. However, during the game she had relaxed and was able to provide her own reassurance by saying: 'Nothing will happen. It will be all right . . .'

Finally, we dealt with the letter to her parents which she had started by saying:

> Dear Mother and Dad,
> I would like to write to you to let you know how I have been feeling, and to reflect a little on the way in which you brought me up . . .

She had gone on to say that she felt very angry and that, while realizing they had given her opportunities, she also thought she had been prevented from taking up many possible options. In addition, she felt her confidence had suffered from the restrictive atmosphere in which she had been brought up.

Jenny had written the letter (a long one) soon after the previous session and had spent much of the week thinking about it. After reading the letter to me, she said, 'I feel I'm coming to grips with some of my feelings about my parents and my nervousness with them, and I'm getting over being intimidated by them. We've always had a parent-child relationship, but I'm now beginning to look at them more as equals.' This was the beginning of her being able honestly to assess her feelings about her parents. Nonetheless, her relationship, with her mother particularly, continued to be a focus of subsequent sessions, when she slowly grew to be more accepting of herself and more confident in her abilities.

SESSION 7.

Jenny began the session by saying:

I've been playing golf with Martin [her husband] and I'm
thoroughly enjoying it. The nervousness seems to be going with
practice . . . I've also been attempting to walk down the street from
our house on my own, taking one house at a time . . . trying to do it
slowly and calmly. I can go to the local shop much more easily now,
but I go there in the car. It's much harder to walk in the street by
myself. I feel the panic rising up inside me and try to quell it by
slowing down and taking deep breaths. On two occasions I've
returned home without getting as far as I wanted to, but I've tried
again on the next day.

I also went to lunch with a friend. She was entertaining in her
own home and was casually dressed, and I felt slightly awkward as I
was overdressed. She's the wife of an executive in the company and
I feel inferior. I guess that's part of learning to sort myself out . . . to
accept that I can be equal. I'm not sure I'll ever change on that
front . . . I've been thinking back, and I realize I was never given any
encouragement or example. I feel sad about it. My father never took
any interest in the things I used to do: sport and so on, and I
remember one year I wanted to learn singing, but he discouraged
it . . . I think it was their way of moulding me into what they wanted
me to be. The daughter he wanted was someone who worked
locally. I didn't go along with that. I remember when I finally moved
closer into London, when I bought the flat, there was tremendous
friction . . . I didn't realize I was so restricted when I was younger. I
just went along with it. I don't feel very angry about it now, as I
think in some ways it was what he thought was best for me. My
mother likewise. She was the stronger of the two. She took too
much interest in some ways, whereas Dad took too little.

. . . In my marriage as well there have been difficulties in
assertiveness. I sometimes feel like saying to Martin 'What about
getting such and such done' (the front fence has needed fixing for
about six months). But then I think 'No, I shouldn't be demanding.
He'll do it in his own time. After all, he's busy with his job.' I
sometimes end up doing it myself, which is OK, but it happens a

lot . . . On the financial side, things are a bit sticky, too. I earn more than he does and when we met he was paying maintenance and never seemed to have much. Also, his priorities are different from mine. He enjoys his cigarettes and drink, whereas I'd rather buy new clothes (when I can get into a shop!) and go to the theatre (which I can't do at present). So, there's been friction from time-to-time on that front . . . Our sex life hasn't suffered though. There don't seem to be problems in that area. We both enjoy it most of the time . . .

The first phase of therapy was focused, as you can see, on establishing the techniques with which to cope with the panic, and talking through many of the issues that contributed to the underlying tension. In parallel with discussion of the broader issues, Jenny was attempting regularly to tackle something new: walking around the block slowly and calmly; practising driving to the corner shop and standing for longer periods at the counter; going to the hairdresser again; once back at work being more assertive with her boss; practising the autogenic methods of relaxation on her way to work in the car and in the office; asking people to lunch, etc. After ten meetings, approximately once-weekly (a couple of the later ones were once a fortnight), the sessions were decreased in frequency to once a month. Then I was away for a further month and she did well during that time. Eventually, sessions were once every two months, until completion of therapy. At the 'half-way' point, during the first month's break in sessions, Jenny wrote to me saying:

I am pleased to be able to write you this note because I know you will be happy to receive it . . . Since I last saw you, I have been feeling better in myself and have therefore wanted to do more. I have had lunch (outside our office building) with three different girlfriends, and had a very enjoyable dinner with Martin at a super restaurant in Covent Garden to celebrate our wedding anniversary. Initially I felt nervous, but I was able to calm myself and enjoyed the evening. But the best achievement of all was last Wednesday afternoon. I had been to the hairdresser's, finished there early and decided to go to the large shopping complex a mile or so from our home. I do not go there very often and on the odd occasion I have

147

gone it has been with Martin. But this was by *myself*. I parked the car, walked into the huge building, went up the escalators to level four and, as you can imagine, by this time I was feeling ten feet tall. I was half expecting something to happen, but I went slowly and took deep breaths and found myself actually enjoying it. After spending half an hour or so shopping at the main department store I proceeded through the mall, went into various shops, tried on two dresses, got a tape and bought a pair of socks for Martin. You can imagine how I felt by this time – just elated. I still cannot believe I did all that and felt so good.

On the way home, I stopped at another shop and ordered two lampshades I had been wanting for some months, I then went to the butchers (where I had had a nasty panic attack some time ago) and home to tell Martin the news of my adventure. Thinking about it now, it sounds like a fairytale, but it is good to be part of the outside world again. I know every day is not going to be like last Wednesday, but I also know that as time goes by many more days will be like last Wednesday. Next week I am going to a fashion parade and luncheon, and by the time I see you again I hope to have more achievements to report . . .

Jenny continued to progress until she required no further sessions. In response to a follow-up questionnaire asking how she was getting on, she responded that she was greatly improved and that:

I have no more panic attacks, much less fear in agoraphobic situations, a return of self-confidence and less reliance on other people . . . I can now go shopping and eat out, and I cope much better with my work. Being able to discuss my problems with someone I feel truly understands and wants to help has helped me a lot. Having set 'goals' to succeed in has been important. I think the treatment covered every aspect it could . . . I need to continue to learn to live comfortably with myself, to pursue my own 'lifestyle management', and continue working on the changes I have made.

Both Liz and Peter (whose life histories are discussed in Chapter 3) were treated in a similar fashion. Both learnt strategies needed to counteract the panic. Both were able gradually to go back into situations they had been avoiding. Both began to be assertive with their spouses, and Peter's new-found ability to be so at work resulted in him being offered a long-overdue promotion. Liz went back to further study and was contemplating part-time work when the ferrying of her children ceased being as arduous. Her relationship with her husband continued to be a problem as she felt he seemed to enjoy putting her down and didn't want her to succeed. She felt that everything she did was not quite good enough for him. He expected her to ask for help, whilst taking pride in not needing help from anyone else himself. She found the whole dynamic of their relationship demoralizing. Marital sessions were necessary for the two of them to talk through these aspects of their relationship. Some changes were made, but Liz remained ambivalent about the situation. Her efforts were directed towards becoming more independent herself, so that she could become less affected by his attitude. As she did so, their relationship improved as she became less nagging than previously for the emotional support she required from him. He became less threatened and less withdrawn, providing her with some of the in-put she required. The situation remained far from ideal, but her own perception of being trapped receded as she worked on the symptoms and gained further independence. In response to the follow-up questionnaire she responded:

I feel now that I know basically what the problem is. Understanding that panic is an over-reaction of the mind and body does help, as does knowing that other people suffer from it and do get well. Relaxation is important . . . I rarely feel agoraphobic now and move around more freely these days.

. . . Understanding agoraphobia, relaxation, talking through my problems, and trying to experiment with ways of handling them have helped me to improve significantly.

## Chapter 14

# Summary

In summary, the framework of treatment outlined in the previous chapters is as follows:

Explanation and understanding of how agoraphobia develops

Developing insight into the underlying tensions in your own life which led to the agoraphobia

Learning strategies to help cope with the panic (e.g. relaxation, counteracting the thoughts)

Tackling the situations and feelings previously avoided at your own pace

Working through the issues underlying the symptoms (be they marital difficulties, unresolved mourning, anger with parents, break-up of a relationship, etc.)

Developing greater self acceptance and self confidence

For each person the framework remains largely the same, though the context may differ. Each person needs to learn to counteract and cope with their symptoms in an essentially similar fashion; but the underlying issues are unique to each individual and they need to be approached and tackled in different ways.

Thus, if there are problems in your marriage, then marital therapy or counselling may be an appropriate way of working through these. If there are individual difficulties, then individual therapy may help you to resolve them. If assertion seems to be a problem, then an assertiveness training course may be of use. It is vital to choose, and embrace, what is appropriate for you. However, it is also important that therapy is not used as a means of escape from the practical problems of learning to cope with the panic and tackling things you have been avoiding.

In dealing with the causes, therapy should be undertaken in parallel with facing the other issues; but, sometimes, it is only when panic ceases to be an all-preoccupying concern that additional matters can be worked on adequately. In this case, coping with the panic may need to be tackled first, though, ideally, it is best for both aspects of treatment to be dealt with in tandem, as one may help the other. Indeed, if you are in therapy and your therapist or counsellor does not deal directly with the panic and avoidance, then you must try to do so yourself; the guidelines provided in this book indicate various ways in which you can start. Although it is not always necessary to discuss the underlying issues with a professional, this can help. Similarly, professional support can be of particular use in assisting you to follow the specific techniques needed to counteract panic and avoidance. Because it helps to have someone with whom you can talk things through, if you find yourself unable to call on a friend or a local self-help group within your community, then sound out what professional help is available and refer yourself. It may even be worthwhile asking your counsellor to read this book if you feel the approach outlined here is one that might be useful, as it is important that the two of you have a clear and mutual understanding about the rationale and aims of treatment. The book could provide a useful starting point.

During and following treatment, many of my patients have outlined to me various things that have helped them, and how they have changed. Some of their comments are outlined below:

### David: 26 years old, agoraphobic for 4 years
I am completely better. My improvement could be summed up by saying I very rarely think about the problem and I don't have any symptoms. I'm now able to drive on freeways and look down from heights – things I used to find impossible . . . I don't think there was one particular aspect of treatment that helped me, except maybe when you told me that when the attacks came they would not harm me. Therefore it was easier to fight them off saying over and over to myself 'It can't hurt me'. Eventually I could control them. Overall, the treatment helped me greatly . . . My main goal now is to fly. I haven't had the opportunity so far, so that is still a task to be tackled ahead of me.

*Keith: 39 years old, agoraphobic for 5 years (discussed in Chapter 1)*
I have improved significantly. I am now able to travel by public
transport more easily and there has been a general decrease in my
anxiety level. I have flown interstate for an interview, which I wouldn't
have been able to do before. It went fine . . . I am now able to tackle
most of the things I previously avoided with a decrease in anxiety. All
of these need continued practice and I need to build up my self
concept in doing so. General discussion in therapy, and confrontation
with a rational understanding of the anxiety has helped me to improve.

*Margaret: 37, agoraphobic for 3 years, mother of 2*
I feel I now know how to relax when I feel panic come on: I breathe
deeply. But really, I have just adjusted my mind to work out not to be
frightened and not to panic. I'm not saying I'm over it completely, but
I'm trying, and I feel I'm doing quite nicely.

    . . . I've been stuck in a lift and I coped really well . . . a great step
forward I thought. My heart was racing, but I paced my mind . . . I can
now go to restaurants and I enjoy going. The same with the cinema. I
have been able to sit in the hairdresser's without feeling I have to get
away. Also, I have a job two days per week which takes me into town by
van with someone else driving. I then go into high-rise buildings to
water the plants. I'm on my own, so no one else can help me; I've had
to do it all myself, and best of all, I'm doing it! I've also had to walk
through the city. The things that have helped are: relaxation, especially
yoga, also to know how the panic is brought on. I like the phrase 'the
fear of fear itself' as I never thought of it that way before. It also helps
to be able now to distinguish between actually feeling a bit off and
sick, and feeling that way because I've told myself I'm sick. To know
that help is available helps . . . Now that I'm able to talk about the
problems I've had, so many people have told me they suffer something
similar. At present I have two close friends who are in a bad way, and
hopefully I'm giving them some help and support . . . I have become
more positive towards myself. I've now realized that I'm not alone or
'off my head'. I'm glad no doctors gave me pills and that I haven't
taken tablets, as that only dulls the problem and it doesn't go away by
itself. You need to tackle it . . . I still need to work on getting rid of my
'what if? . . .' attitude, but I'm feeling a lot more positive about things.

# Summary

*Sarah: 29 years old, agoraphobic for 4 years*

I now understand my problems and most times can handle a potential panic attack. I can also now do simple things like shopping and driving and going to the hairdresser's without stress. I have learned, too, how damaging stress can be and I feel slightly more capable of controlling my feelings . . . I think what has helped most of all is the security of knowing and understanding the effects of agoraphobia, and knowing how to cope with it. The benefits of relaxing, seeing why it happened in the first instance, and learning to know more about myself have all been important. I still have to work on goals of feeling even more fully in control, making my life more fulfilling and developing my confidence.

*Mark: 31 years old, agoraphobic for 6 years*

I continue to experience some increase of tension in prolonged time outside alone, but the severe symptoms have disappeared. I can go out whenever I like, without fear that severe symptoms will appear, especially later in the day. I still find the mornings slightly more difficult. Certain types of shopping are still stressful, but I no longer have any problems at supermarkets. Restaurants and bars are easier, and cinemas are no problem at all . . . The agoraphobic symptoms seem to have decreased/disappeared with a general lowering of tension. Relaxation exercises and mild exercise (e.g. walking) have helped; also, the establishment of a work and relaxation routine, and organizing my time better. The examination of my earlier experiences with family and friends, and the relation of this to my present means of coping in difficult situations with people, has been very helpful. Also, the revelation that some of these situations are produced by myself. There are still goals I need to work on, for example smoking and drinking as means of quelling tension. I also want to work on the general issues of self-confidence and self-respect . . .

*Helen: 29 years old, agoraphobic for 3 1/2 years*

When I look into the future I am far more confident that it will be better than I could have imagined a while ago. I am slowly becoming more sure of myself in many ways . . . In the past few weeks I've travelled further than I have for years and visited three large regional shopping centres during the school holidays when they were crowded. My husband now frequently wonders where I'm off to on my jaunts away from our farm, as he's so used to me staying home all the time. He's delighted with my improvement . . . Having someone regularly reviewing my progress is an incentive to keep practising and to try to make going out a habit. The discussions and letter-writing concerning my relationship with my mother had a major effect on my improvement. The recommended reading is also helpful, as is keeping the diary. I'm very happy with the results of treatment. My main aim now is to travel overseas again and to be able to enjoy myself, and not be a burden to my husband. This is much better than it was.

*Bruce: 35 years old, agoraphobic for 18 months*
I have greatly improved, but I must emphasize that the improvement to normal life again took almost 18 months. I was surprised at how long it can take to really feel *normal* again. I have been able to resume life as it was prior to my condition developing. I'm back to normal . . .

Understanding the reason behind what I called *stress* attacks (known to you as panic attacks), helped tremendously. Once I learned how and why the body reacts to certain situations, I began to realize that these panic (or stress) attacks have been coming and going since I was a child. However, I had never experienced one in an exaggerated form as I did just prior to coming for treatment. This was explained to me, and that was the turning point to recovery . . . I also found that improving physical fitness was important and having increased sleep at night. Diet was also important as adrenalin tires you out. (I found a tremendous improvement after taking Pantothonic Acid B6 found naturally in Royal Jelly.) . . . I must say that I was fortunate to have a GP who was able to recognize the problem and refer me for appropriate treatment instead of prescribing drugs which would probably have solved the problem in the short term only and created a much larger long-term problem . . . Now, my aim is continued good health, and the need to not let this situation develop again is of paramount importance. It is also important to have confidence in one's ability to control a stress situation, should it arise again.

*Mary: (discussed in Chapters 9, 10, and 12) 43 years old, agoraphobic for 18 months*

My anxiety level has dropped considerably and I feel more relaxed. When I am out and I feel anxiety coming on, I have learnt not to panic. I have learnt how to control my anxious feelings. I am also gradually coming off my tablets and am now down to a third of what I was on before. Only one more to go . . . I am able to go into supermarkets now, chat to people, and stand in queues and not panic. Or, if I do, I can control it. I am also able to go out to dinner, yoga and church. I still think about where I am going before I go. It doesn't come naturally yet. I still have to force myself to do certain things. But I can do it, and I'm pleased about that, and I'm working towards the day, which I feel is coming, when I just get up and do it . . . To be told what was wrong with me was very important, and then learning how to deal with the problem was crucial. Knowing what all those dreadful feelings were, being motivated into doing things, doing them, and gaining confidence to do it again and again until it becomes easier each time: all of these things helped. I know I am getting well, and I know a lot of getting well is up to me too . . . It has been helpful to *talk* to someone who knows how you are feeling. Also, it has helped to understand my problem and to learn how to deal with it, to be motivated to do things you don't think that you can do, and to gain confidence and to feel better about yourself and the people around you. Thinking positively about things helps, and knowing that one day soon you are going to feel how you used to feel before you got agoraphobia . . . I still want to work on lots of things. I would like to be completely off all tablets, and I want to be able to do all the things I want without thinking about it: just to get up and go. I would also like to feel less tired, and to be able to cope with all life's ups and downs – again without tablets. Basically, I want to be happy and well, and I'm well on the way to getting there.

*Katherine: (discussed in Chapter 1) 52 years old, agoraphobic for 27 years*
I am able to cope better with my panic feelings, and I can now work part-time and go out shopping and enjoy it. I can also go to Rotary dinners with my husband which I enjoy. Being taught to understand my bad feelings and how to cope with them helped. I find that the deep breathing and relaxing of my body when I get myself uptight

helps a lot. I have learned a lot about myself and have also learned to cope with my relationship with my husband. My main aim now is to develop more confidence in being able to go to places on my own and to be able to be fully independent. I can now drive my own car, so I am well on the way to these goals.

*Frances: (discussed in Chapter 12) 60 years old, agoraphobic for 4 years*
There is so much more I can do now than I was able to do when I first came for treatment. I am now able to leave the house, go shopping, go visiting, drive the car, eat out, go to the pictures and small theatre groups and ride on a bus. I am also able to go for a holiday and visit my daughter. The relaxation tape has been helpful, although it is not always easy to put it into practice. Having the condition explained to you so that you can understand what is happening to you and why is also important. I found my setback very difficult [discussed in Chapter 12], but after that I have continued to improve . . . I was just so pleased to find that there was help available . . . As I have said, I think to understand the condition is the first step towards recovery. I have also found the books on the subject a great help, particularly the one by Dr Weekes. I've also found an agoraphobic self-help group that I have joined of benefit. I still have goals I want to work on. The ultimate would be to conquer flying, and I'm working towards it.

*Rebecca: 25 years old, agoraphobic for 2 years*
I'm more confident and relaxed with people and a lot happier. I can now go to work and go into any shops I want without feeling nervous. Understanding why I have it and knowing it is not uncommon have helped me tremendously.

*Shirley: 58 years old, agoraphobic for 10 years*
I am now able to go shopping with confidence, deal with the traffic and with shop assistants, and I'm able to go out again on my own. I previously couldn't. Realizing that I'm not the only person who has suffered these feelings has helped tremendously, as has reading books about 'self improvement' (such as Claire Weekes' books; also *The Erroneous Zones* and *When I Say No I Feel Guilty*). I have changed a lot and now feel much freer. My main aim is 'to be liberated!' and to continue working towards whatever I feel like doing to make my life more fulfilling and interesting.

All of these people have improved. Some completed therapy a while ago, others are still continuing with it. Some are using the help of family and friends in assisting them to achieve their goals of going out, shopping, driving, travelling by public transport. Others are doing it on their own. The important thing is that they understand what has happened to them and what to do about it. Some do it quickly, others do it at a more gradual pace. You will find that these techniques work for you, too. You may well find that you need someone to support you through the process and, if so, call on a friend or professional counsellor who is understanding of your needs.

What you will definitely need is the wish to get well, the motivation and determination to succeed and the courage to face and ride through the anxiety. Ultimately, you are the only one who can overcome the problem. You are your own most valuable resource, so learn to use your abilities and to help yourself. If you are determined to succeed and get better, you will make it. So . . . TAKE COURAGE, AND GO FOR IT.

# Appendix A

# Self-Help Book List

The following list of books are those which were found useful by my own patients and/or are recommended by other colleagues. The books have been classified with regard to particular problems, or areas of growth. Within each section the books are ordered alphabetically by author. Where followed by 'pb', the edition is available in paperback. *Asterisks refer to warmly recommended books.

## Agoraphobia

### A. SELF-HELP REFERENCES

*Clarke, J. C. and Wardman, W. (1985): *Agoraphobia: A Clinical and Personal Account*, Pergamon Press, (Australia), pb

Frampton, Muriel (1984): *Agoraphobia: Coping with the World Outside*, Turnstone Press Ltd, UK

*Mathews, A. M., Gelder, M. G. and Johnston, D. W. (1981): *Programmed Practice for Agoraphobia*: i) Client's Manual, ii) Partner's Manual, Tavistock Publications, London, pb

McKinnon, Pauline (1983): *In Stillness Conquer Fear*, Dove Communications, Melbourne, pb

Mitchell, Ross (1982): *Phobias*, Penguin, London, pb

Neville, Alice (1986): *Who's Afraid of Agoraphobia?*, Century Arrow, London, pb

Vosc, Ruth Hurst (1981): *Agoraphobia*, Faber & Faber Ltd, London, pb

*Weekes, Claire (1977): *Agoraphobia: Simple Effective Treatment*, Angus & Robertson, London

### B. THEORETICAL REFERENCES

Chambless, D. L., and Goldstein, A. J. (eds.) (1982): *Agoraphobia: Multiple Perspectives on Theory and Treatment*, John Wiley & Sons, New York

Mathews, A. M., Gelder, M. G. and Johnston, D. W. (1981): *Agoraphobia: Nature and Treatment*, Tavistock Publications, London

Thorpe, Geoffrey L. and Burns, Laurence E. (1983): *The Agoraphobic Syndrome: Behavioural Approaches to Evaluation and Treatment*, Wiley, Chichester

# Assertion and Social Skills

Alberti, Robert E., and Emmons, Michael (1970): *Your Perfect Right: A Guide to Assertive Living*, Impact Publications, California, pb

Dickson, Anne (1983): *A Woman in Your Own Right*, Quartet, London, pb

Fensterheim, H. and Baer, J. (1976): *Don't Say Yes When You Want to Say No*, Futura, pb

Hauck, Paul (1981): *How to Stand up for Yourself*, Sheldon Press, pb

Jakubowski, Patricia and Lange, Arthur J. (1978): *The Assertive Option: Your Rights and Responsibilities*, Research Press Co, Illinios, pb

Smith, M. J. (1975): *When I Say No I Feel Guilty*, Bantam Books, pb

Zimbardo, P. (1980): *Shyness*, Pan, pb


# Working Towards Growth

*Dyer, Wayne (1977): *Your Erroneous Zones*, Sphere, pb (emphasizes areas such as self-respect, approval seeking, guilt and worry)

Dyer, Wayne (1979): *Pulling Your Own Strings*, Hamlyn, pb (sequel to *Your Erroneous Zones*, emphasizes assertion)

*Ellis, A. and Harper, R. (1978): *A New Guide to Rational Living*, Wilshire Book Co., California, pb (a good introduction to working on counter-productive thoughts)

Ernst, S. and Goodison, L. (1981): *In Your Own Hands: A Book of Self-Help Therapy*, The Women's Press, pb

*Fensterheim, H. and Baer, J. (1976): *Don't Say Yes When You Want to Say No*, Futura, pb (a good introduction to the philosophy of behaviour therapy; also good on assertion)

Hodgson, Ray and Miller, Peter (1980): *Self-Watching: Addiction, Habits, Compulsions and What to do About Them*, Century Publishing, London

Kassorla, Irene (1977): *Putting It All Together*, Circus Books, N.Y., pb

Lazarus, A. and Fay, A. (1975): *I Can If I Want To*, Warner Books, pb

Orlick, Terry (1980): *In Pursuit of Excellence*, Human Kinectics Publishers Inc

Priestley, P., McGuire, J., Flegg, D., Hemsley. V. and Welham, D. (1978): *Social Skills and Personal Problem Solving: A Handbook of Methods*, Tavistock Publications, London, pb

Mahoney, M. J., (1979): *Self Change*, Norton

Raynor, C. (1980): *Everything Your Doctor Would Tell You If He Had The Time*, Pan, pb

Robinson, D. and Henry, S. (1977): *Self-Help and Health: Mutual Aid for Modern Problems*, Chaucer Press, pb (a survey of self-help groups and analysis of the modern phenomenon of Self-Help)

Robinson, D. and Robinson, Y. (1979): *From Self-Help to Health: A Guide to Self-Help Groups*, Concord Books, London

Vickery, D. M. *et al* (1980): *Take care of Yourself*, Unwin, pb

# Relationships

Rubin, Lillian (1983): *Intimate Strangers: What Goes Wrong in Relationships Today – and Why*, Fontana, pb

# Women's Issues

*Dowling, Colette (1981): *The Cinderella Complex: Women's Hidden Fear of Independence*, Fontana, pb

Fransella, Fay and Fros, Kay (1977): *Women: On Being A Woman: A Review of Research on how Women see Themselves*. Tavistock Publications, London, pb

*Rubin, Lillian B. (1979): *Women of a Certain Age: The Midlife Search for Self*, Harper & Row, USA

Russianoff, Penelope (1985): *Why Do I Think I Am Nothing Without A Man?*, Bantam Books

Scarf, Maggie (1980): *Unfinished Business: Pressure Points in the Lives of Women*, Fontana, pb

Seaman, Florence and Lorimer, Anne (1979): *Winning at Work: A Book for Women*, Running Press, Philadelphia, USA

Graham Yates, Gayle (1975): *What Women Want*, Harvard University Press, pb

# Relaxation

Jacobson, Edmund (1936): *You Must Relax*, McGraw-Hill

Walker, C. E. (1975): *Learn to Relax*, Prentice Hall (Spectrum), pb (a general guide to relaxation)

# Sex

Barbach, L. (1976): *For Yourself*, Anchor Books, pb

Brown, P. (1979): *Treat Yourself to Sex*, Penguin, pb

Comfort, Alex (1972): *The Joy of Sex*, Simon & Schuster

Comfort, Alex (1977): *More Joy of Sex*, Quartet, pb

Devlin, D. (1974): *The Book of Love*, New English Library, pb

Devlin, D. (1976): *Carefree Love*, New English Library, pb

*Heimen, J., Lopiccolo, L. and Lopiccolo, J. (1976): *Becoming Orgasmic*, Prentice Hall (Spectrum), pb

Katchadourian, H. (1974): *Human Sexuality*, W. H. Freeman, pb

Reuben, D. (1970): *Everything You Wanted to Know About Sex*, W. H. Allen pb

# Anxiety and Stress

Charlesworth, Edward A. and Nathan, Ronald G. (1986): *Stress Management: A Comprehensive Guide to Wellness*, Souvenir Press, London, pb

Lawson, Alethe (1978): *Freedom from Stress*, Thorsons, pb

Marks, Isaac (1979): *Living with Fear*, McGraw-Hill, pb

\*Message, J. (1986): *A Practical Guide to Stress and its Management*, Century Hutchinson, Melbourne, pb

Parrino, John J. (1979): *From Panic to Power*, John Wiley & Sons, New York

\*Weekes, Claire (1981): *Self Help for Your Nerves*, Angus & Robertson, pb

Weekes, Claire (1981): *Peace from Nervous Suffering*, Angus & Robertson, pb

Woolfolk, R. L. and Richardson, F. C. (1979): *Stress, Sanity and Survival*, Futura, pb

# Depression

\*Beck, A.T. and Greenberg, R. L. (1978): *Coping with Depression*, pb (available from Centre for Cognitive Therapy, University of Pensylvania, USA)

Burns, David D. (1980): *Feeling Good: The New Mood Therapy*, Signet Publishers, pb

De Rosis, Helen A. (1976): *The Book of Hope: How Women Can Overcome Depressian*, Bantam, pb

Dominian, Jack (1976): *Depression: What is it? How do we Cope?*, Fontana, pb

Jensen, E. A. (1981): *Depression Challenges*, pb (recommended by Depressives Associated, and available for £3.50 from 6 Attree Drive, Queen's Park, Brighton, BN2 2HN, UK)

Juniper, Dean (1978): *How to Lift Your Depression*, Open Books, London, pb

\*Nairne, Kathy and Smith, Gerrilyn (1984): *Dealing with Depression*, Women's Press, London, pb

Rowe, Dorothy (1983): *Depression: The Way Out of Your Prison*, Routledge & Kegan Paul, London, pb

Sanders, Deirdre (1984): *Women and Depression*, Sheldon Press, London, pb

\*Scarf, Maggie (1980): *Unfinished Business: Pressure Points in the Lives of Women*, Fontana, pb

Watts, C. A. H. (1980): *Defeating Depression: A Guide for Depressed People and Their Families*, Thorsons, UK, pb

# Bereavement

McNeil Taylor, Liz (1983): *Living with Loss*, Fontana, pb

## Obesity/Weight Issues

Cannon, Geoffrey and Enzig, Hetty (1983): *Dieting Makes You Fat: A Guide to Energy, Food, Fitness and Health*, Sphere Books, pb
Orbach, Susie (1978): *Fat is a Feminist Issue*, Hamlyn, pb

## Gynaecological

Dennerstein, Lorrain, Wood, Carl and Burrows, Graham (1982): *Hysterectomy: How to Deal with the Physical and Emotional Aspects*, Oxford University Press
Rayner, Claire (1977): *Pregnancy*, BBC Books

## *Appendix B*

# Supplementary Treatment Aids

There are now a great many treatment aids available, notably audio-cassettes and records as well as written material:

a. Three self-help cassettes are available from the author:

   i.  Relaxation: *Progressive Relaxation Exercises* (long form) and *Autogenic Relaxation Exercises* (short form)

   ii.  The Treatment of Agoraphobia: Learning to Cope with Panic

   iii.  Building Your Confidence and Self Esteem

   For further information, send a stamped addressed envelope to: P.O. Box 700, Hawthorn, 3122, Melbourne, Victoria, Australia.

b. Dr Claire Weekes' cassettes and records are available from: 16 Rivermead Court, Ranelagh Gardens, London, SW6 3RT, UK.

c. A series of booklets on the management of stress: *A Guided Self-Management Series for Stress-Related Disorders* is available from the Western Center Health Group, P.O. Box 91542, Vancouver, B.C., Canada, V7V3P2.

d. Also of use are the two treatment manuals (for clients and partners) by Mathews, Gelder and Johnston (in the self-help references on agoraphobia).

## Appendix C

# Resources for Psychological Treatment of Agoraphobia, and Self-Help Groups

**Treatment**: Contact the psychology department of a central (well-reputed) teaching hospital to obtain information about where psychological therapy for agoraphobia is available. It is important to go to someone with specific expertise in the area.

Mind (National Association for Mental Health), 22 Harley Street, London, WIN 2ED, will give advice and information, both with regard to resources for psychological treatment of agoraphobia in and around London and the UK, and self-help groups.

Community-based facilities also frequently offer expert help for agoraphobia. For example, in Australia: The Cairnmillar Institute, 993 Burke Road, Camberwell, 3124, offers a phobia clinic providing specialized help in the area. It is important to seek out these pockets of expertise if you are going for treatment.

**Self-help groups**: Again, an up-to-date list of self-help groups in Britain can be obtained through Mind (address above). Several of the better known ones are:

Relaxation for Living,
29 Burwood Park Road,
Walton-on-Thames,
Surrey. (Send s.a.e. for information)

Yoga for Health Foundation,
Ickwell Bury,
Biggleswade,
Bedfordshire, SG18 9EF.

Pre-Menstrual Tension Advisory Service,
P.O. Box 268,
Hove,
Sussex, BN3 IRW.

The Nottingham and County Phobic Association,
c/o 1 Oban Road,
Chilwell,
Nottingham.

*In Australia*:

The Agoraphobia Support Group,
P.O. Box 98,
Ascot Vale,
Victoria, 3032. (Tel: 03-5283492)

The Shepparton Support Group,
c/o 28 Vickers Street,
Kialla,
Victoria, 3631.

A.S.H.O.G. 39 Darghan Street,
Glebe,
New South Wales, 2037. (Tel: 02-6606136)

The Southern Districts Agoraphobia Centre INC.
88 Dyson Road,
Christies Beach,
South Australia, 5165. (Tel: 08-3826055)

# Notes

CHAPTER 1

1. Buglass, D., Clarke, J., Henderson, A. S., Kreitman, N., and Presley, A. S. (1977): 'A study of agoraphobic housewives', *Psychological Medicine*, 7, pp 73–86
2. Agras, W. S., Sylvester, D., and Oliveau, D. (1969): 'The Epidemiology of common fears and phobias', *Comprehensive Psychiatry*, 10, pp 151–56
3. Quoting Dr Jerry Kasdorf, founder and clinical director of the Phobia Care Treatment Center in Santa Ana, Fallerton, Huntingdon Beach and Colton, USA. (Tel: (714) 547 2400.) Interviewed in *Household Magazine*, July 1985
4. Marks, I. M. and Herst, E. R. (1970): 'A survey of 1,200 agoraphobics in Britain', *Social Psychiatry*, 5, pp 16–24
5. Brehony, Kathleen A. and Scott Geller, E. (1981): 'Agoraphobia: Appraisal of Research and a Proposal for an Integrative Model', *Behaviour Research and Therapy*, Vol. 12, pp 2–66
6. Shafar, Susanne (1976): 'Aspects of Phobic Illness: A Study of 90 personal cases', *British Journal of Medical Psychology*, 49, pp 221–36
7. Tearnan, B. H., Telch, M. J. and Keefe, P. (1984): 'Etiology and Onset of Agoraphobia: A Critical Review', *Comprehensive Psychiatry*, Vol. 25, pp 1, 51–62
8. Mathews, Andrew M., Gelder, Michael. G., and Johnston, D. W. (1981): 'Agoraphobia: Nature and Treatment', *Tavistock Publications*, London


CHAPTER 2

1. Fodor, I. G. (1974): 'The Phobic Syndrome in Women' in V. Franks and V. Burke (eds): *Women in Therapy*, Brunner/Mazel, New York
2. Emmelkamp, P. M. G. (1979): 'The behavioural study of clinical phobias' in Hersen, M., Eisler, R. M. and Miller, P. M., *Progress in Behaviour Modification*, Volume 8, pp 55–125 Academic Press, New York


CHAPTER 5

1. Snaith, R. P. (1968): 'A clinical investigation of phobias', *British Journal of Psychiatry*, 114, pp 673–98 (he studied a group of 27 agoraphobics)

2. Webster, A. S. (1953): 'The development of phobias in married women', *Psychological Monographs*, 67, pp 1–18
3. Marks, I. M., and Gelder, M. G. (1965): 'A controlled retrospective study of behaviour therapy in phobic patients', *British Journal of Psychiatry*, 111, pp 561–73
4. Bowlby, J. (1973): *Attachment and Loss, Volume II, Separation, Anxiety and Anger*, Hogarth Press, London
5. Solyom, L., Beck, P., Solyom, C. *et al* (1974): 'Some etiological factors in phobic neurosis', *Canadian Psychiatric Association Journal*, 19, pp 69–77; and
   Solyom, L., Sieberfeld, M. and Solyom, C. (1976): 'Maternal overprotection in the etiology of agoraphobia', *Canadian Psychiatric Association Journal*, 21, pp 109–113
6. Tearnan *et al* (*see* note 7., Chapter 1)
7. Ibid
8. Bandura, A. (1977): 'Social learning theory', Prentice-Hall, Englewood Cliffs, N.J.
9. Rimm, D. C., Janda, L. H., Lancaster, D. W., Nahl, M., and Dittman, K. (1977): 'An exploratory investigation of the origin and maintenance of phobias', *Behaviour Research and Therapy*, 15, pp 231–38
10. Goldstein, A. J. and Chambless, D. L. (1978): 'A reanalysis of agoraphobia', *Behaviour Therapy*, 9, pp 47–59
11. Stampler, F. M. (1982): 'Panic Disorder: Description, Conceptualization and Implications for Treatment', *Clinical Psychology Review*, Vol. 2, pp 469–86.
12. Andrews, I. D. (1966): 'Psychotherapy of Phobias', *Psychological Bulletin*, 66, pp 455–80
13. Emmelkamp, P. M. G. and Cohen-Kettenis, P. (1975): 'Relationship of locus of control to phobic anxiety and depression', *Psychological Reports*, 36, pp 390–91
14. Goldstein, A. J. (1973): 'Learning theory insufficiency in understanding agoraphobia – a plea for empiricism', in Brengelmann, J. C. and Tanner, W. (eds): *Proceedings of the European Association for Behaviour Therapy and Modification, 1971*, Urban and Schwarzenberg, Munich
15. Goldstein, A. J. and Chambless, D. L. (1978) (see note 10 above)
16. Hafner, R. J. (1977): 'The husbands of agoraphobic women: Assortative mating or pathogenic interaction?', *British Journal of Psychiatry*, 130, pp 233–39
17. e.g. Holmes, J. (1982): 'Phobia and counterphobia: Family aspects of agoraphobia', *Journal of Family Therapy*, 4, pp 133–52

CHAPTER 6

1. Liebowitz, M. R. and Klein, D. F. (1982): 'Agoraphobia: Clinical Features, Pathophysiology and Treatment' in Chambless, D. L. and Goldstein, A. J. (eds): *Agoraphobia: Multiple Perspectives on theory and treatment*, John Wiley & Sons, New York
2. Lader, M. and Mathews, A. M. (1970): 'Physiological changes during spontaneous panic attacks', *Journal of Psychosomatic Research*, 14, pp 377–82
3. Redmond, D. E. (1979): 'New and old evidence for the involvement of a brain norepinephrine system in anxiety', in Fann, W. E., Karacan, I., Pokorny, A. D. and Williams, R. L. (eds): *Phenomenology and Treatment of Anxiety*, Spectrum Publications, New York
4. Stampler p 474 (*see* note 11., Chapter 5)
5. Tearnan *et al* (*see* note 7., Chapter 1)


CHAPTER 7

1. D. S. M. III: *American Psychiatric Association: Diagnostic and Statistical Manual of Mental Disorders*, Third Edition. Washington D.C., APA, 1980, pp 226–7
2. Brehony and Scott Geller (*see* note 4., Chapter 1)


CHAPTER 9

1. Fodor I. G. (*see* note 1., Chapter 2)


CHAPTER 10

1. In: Neidhardt, E. J., Conry, R. F. and Weinstein, M. S. (1982): *Autogenic Methods: A Guided Self-Management Series for Stress-Related Disorders*, 1982, Western Center for Preventive and Behavioural Medicine Inc.


CHAPTER 11

1. The original source of the Life Line as a method for self-exploration was: Priestley, P., McGuire, J., Flegg, D., Hensley, V., and Welham, D. (1978): *Social Skills and Personal Problem Solving: A Handbook of Methods*, Tavistock Publications, London

# Index